I Barely Got Here!

Can I Make it in Teaching?

Hannah Lynn Demerson

Dedication

This book is dedicated to all the families who entrusted their kids to public school.
And to all their teachers who gave what they could. In some cases, it was negligible.
In most cases, it was epic.
And to all the families who will continue to place their children in our trust: you probably don't think you have a choice. The airlines say, "We know you have a choice in airlines. Thank you for choosing us." In most cases, the students I taught did not have the household income required for private school, nor were their parents able to consider other options like homeschooling. I used to think to myself (I hope I didn't say it out loud too many times) "How many brothers and sisters did you say you have? Because I can't imagine having more at home like you!" But to be fair, there were many I did tell, "I would adopt you in a minute." But that doesn't mean I would homeschool you (wink).
Now that we have entered the era of a pandemic, I will further dedicate this work to the teachers who continue on, undaunted by the need for remote education and all of its challenges and frustrations. I continued to remote homeschool my own grandson, while commiserating with my former colleagues who are facing their fears of going back to the brick-and-mortar schools and the exposure that will impose. My best wishes go with them. And in the wake of the school shootings in Uvalde, Texas, my heart is breaking for the heroes and angels, the parents and family and friends, and those teachers who gave it all.

Contents

Foreword

My sister and I are lucky. We got to have Mrs. Demerson as our first teacher. I still remember sitting at the kitchen table in our first apartment, being patiently shown how to draw the curvy letters of my middle name. Being taught how to defend my human rights: responding to bullies by making a fist, a mean mug, and saying, "giiiit outa my face!" How to build the Parthenon out of Popsicle sticks-- or braid hair.

There is an abundance of things she taught us directly, but the most important lessons we learned by her example. When she started the Feed the World Club at Overfelt High School, I learned that there were children my age, perhaps with dreams just like mine, with friends and families just like mine, but without food, running water, or a school to attend. More importantly, I learned that there was something I could do to help them even if they were halfway around the world. When we went to serve food at the local homeless shelter, I learned that the people with these problems are not only half way around the world. They're my countrymen, my neighbors, and my classmates, and that there is a deep reward in sharing your abundance with others. Hearing the stories of her life as a teacher taught us to respect our own individuality, to respect and appreciate the unique journeys of others, and that you can always dig deeper to open your heart wider. You can always work harder.

Over the years as a high school teacher, Mrs. Demerson worked in some of the most difficult schools with the most challenging students. She looked at the so-called underachievers, criminals, gangsters, welfare moms, and illegals, and she saw children. In that I mean she saw their innocence and their infinite potential. She knew that the kids with the guns are the ones that need the most protecting, and she created space for them to be children. To build dioramas, to draw, to question, to make mistakes and to get second, third, and fourth chances, because she knows there are many paths to success and each of us must find our own. Year after year after year, students would shower her with gifts and gratitude even if they didn't get good grades!

Although a consummate and proud grammarian, she was so much more than an English teacher. She was a social worker if your parents were abusing you, a psychiatrist if you were depressed or lost, a spiritual advisor when the world stopped making sense (as often happens in high school), and a mother if you needed food or clothing.

Although she loves to talk, Mrs. Demerson is a listener. She always invited student voices into the learning process and into her heart. The cholas dress her as one of their own for Halloween because she knows they are much more than a pendlelton and a pair of dickies, and because she allowed them to laugh at themselves by respecting their humanity. The Black student union chose this white woman to be their faculty advisor because they trust and respect her as much as she trusts and respects them. Her students from all over the world want to read because her curriculum honors their cultural identities, their struggles and their dreams.

I never dreamed I would be a teacher, but my first assignment as a substitute teacher in ESUHSD was at Overfelt High School, where my mom taught for many years. It was a special Ed class which I had no preparation for. On the three-minute walk from the office to the classroom, I managed to somehow lose the key, and when I got to the room there was a condom wrapped around the door knob. Perhaps the best teaching strategy I learned from my mom was to stay calm and act like everything is normal, when in fact, nothing is under control. I walked over to the first adult I saw and asked for help. He asked who I was and when I told him, his face lit up. "Oh! You're Mrs. Demerson's daughter!" he said, and helped me get everything arranged. From then on, I proudly wore my title of Ms. Demerson, attempting to follow her legacy. I am truly in awe of her dedication to public education for over 4 decades. After just three years as a middle school teacher in New York I burned out and resigned, so I can't even grasp how she was able to regenerate energy and effort year after year. In more ways than I can name, Mrs. Demerson truly embodied the words of Kahlil Gibran, "work is love made visible." so we salute you Mom for changing lives, one essay at a time!

--Doctor Rainy Consuelo Demerson

Acknowledgements

I could never give thanks enough to the many people who helped me along the way. I could never give thanks enough to my family for what attention they may have had to share with my career, nor could I thank them enough for the love and inspiration. But I shall try. *Thank you*!

Thanks to my editors, Lorreta Sylvestre, Anna K. Lee, and Joan Martin, this book should have many fewer confusing parts! I love what you did for it! Thank you to Kate Reynolds, expert adviser on autism, and lovely Lavender Librarian!

The aides who worked with me always remain in my mind's eye as I think, "What would I have done without my merry band of helpers?" Jennifer Nguyen and Jimmy and Kevin, you know who you are. The brother and sister Johnny and Justina; the Ocampo family; the Nguyen sisters (all honors kids); Richie, Giva, and Sergie; and several other sibling teams took special places in my heart. But do you know why your help meant so much? Because you were funny and kind and so smart, and things got done that saved me countless hours of pain. Sarah and Martin and the other Martin, Benton, and all the rest of my aides, I know I will never be able to repay you. You were the ones who made it possible for me to survive each day and get through to retirement without giving up.

Hailey Moore and John Huynh, what would my last years have been if you had not made my teaching life so crazy? You taped candy under my table, so I couldn't find it and wouldn't eat it. Thank goodness. You threw Vietnamese noodle drink on the floor in front of me in a rage, yet came to clean my house when I couldn't do it anymore. Jessica, I will never forget the hard times and the good times, taking you home to your little trailer and wishing your life's joy could equal the joy you brought to me.

D, when you showed me a six-foot-tall broad-shouldered Latina gangster girl could be as sweet and vulnerable as any fluffy girly tiny freshman, my heart melted. Remember when I told you to leave class and go immediately to Planned Parenthood for the morning after pill? Remember when you thought your hopes for ever finding a husband were dashed because you had that certain condition, and I told you my friend and her husband had it for twenty years with no problems, and it would be fine! Remember when I ran into you years later, you were happily married with a baby girl, and we hugged and cried together with tears of joy?

Clorama and Loretta, what can I do to let you know what it meant to have you come and help me get dolled up for my first dress-up dinner at my husband's work celebration for Mercedes Benz? And to stay my friends as you explore the world, reach out, and show the kids from the East Side that dreams of world travel and careers in arts and expression can come true.

Clorama, what can I say about your cover drawing? It's a perfect depiction of my teaching life!

Miriam and Carina and Yadira, you helped my family, and we hope we helped you, too. You were and always will be those hard-working girls who helped their parents labor for a living, and when it comes time for your rewards, I hope they are all the joys life has to offer, and more. There are so many I am leaving out, but some of these names may find themselves thinking, my teacher was a nut. I hope so. A nut who loved you, nonetheless.

Part I

Chapter 1. Through Tragedy and Comedy

Way back in 1983, having finished my degree and credentialing program, I landed a job teaching high school English in a public school in East San José, California. Sometimes the students would come in late, and of course there were so many excuses that the students and I used to joke about how I would "one day write a book about 'em." My favorite excuse so far came from a Samoan student with a large, picked-out Afro.

"Mrs. Demerson, I know I'm late, but *I couldn't help it! I couldn't find my COMB!*"

Clearly this was a disaster that excused any subsequent misdemeanor. But the classic all-time winner of excuses is the exclamation by students when told they are tardy. *"I barely got here!"* Uh, yeah, that's what "tardy" means. But no. I finally worked out what it meant to the students. That student did not arrive on campus and then intentionally avoid coming specifically to *my* class. On the contrary, the student in question had just arrived on campus (therefore, somehow, not responsible for his own tardiness?) There's a subtle difference there.

I BARELY GOT HERE! = the mantra of those who feel they have been wrongfully detained in the institution called school.

I BARELY GOT HERE! = the feeling new teachers experience-- that they might have walked into the wrong picture.

Rewind three more years to 1980. I was a teaching assistant in a special education classroom in Santa Clara, practicing up for the career I had wanted since second grade. Fifteen minutes after the bell rang, a charming Mexican-American boy sauntered in, hair slicked back, wearing tightly-creased chino pants. He leaned back and challenged: "*¿Qué Pasó?*" (What happened?)

Now why would he ask *me* what happened when *he* was the one who was late! Since I knew that it really meant, "What's going on?" I started to laugh. It struck me then as it does now —a metaphor for the elusive and often comical relationship between what students think is the *Job of the Teacher* versus the *Job of the Student*.

It is the *Job of the Teacher* to be there for them, but their attendance is a gift to us! Don't we recognize how grateful we should be that they have arrived? Learning these things gave me an advantage that is at the very core of how I succeeded in my chosen career—loving it every day the way I always dreamed I would. Kids are funny and in so many ways are not like adults: each one of them is capable of undreamt-of change. Recognizing that the potential for change works, not just within the student, but also within the heart of the teacher, is one of the most important lessons I was able to learn very early on.

Sharing the road through high school with thousands of young people has been a thirty-four-year roller-coaster of a ride filled with agony and delight. As you consider becoming a teacher, or if you just want to learn more about the actual experience, read on. There may be advice to be found, and certainly the truth of my experience.

So you've just arrived in teaching. Knowing about the extra-curricular activities going on *during* your class is key to successful survival. The "other curriculum," as I like to call it, consists of those lessons that students are teaching each other while you are writing on the board or working with someone else's group in what the state loves to call Cooperative Learning.

These "other curriculum" lessons consist of all the things that occupy the adolescent mind—from the upcoming calculus test all the way to gang recruitment. My personal favorite is nonsense: anything silly and funny to them (lord knows, not to us). The key is in knowing when which of these lessons are going on, and what to do or not to do about them.

To do or not to do. That is the question.

These are the kinds of things that can really derail good intentions or forge a great teacher:

1. *Tragedy and Comedy*
2. *Autism*
3. *Learning Gap*
4. *Cheating—Using Your Class for Another Teacher's Work*
5. *Sadness*
6. *Depression*
7. *Drug Use*
8. *Righteous Anger*
9. *Sociopathology*
10. *Mean Girl Syndrome*
11. *Fight Club*
12. *Rapscallions*
13. *Well-Meaning Annoyers*
14. *Pets*
15. *Funny people*
16. *Electronics*
17. *The Purpose for/Bane of Our Existence: Teen Love*
    a.) *Gag Me with a Spoon*
    b.) *Most Beautiful Thing You'll Ever Witness*
    c.) *Relationship Violence*

We must say that gang involvement and recruitment in our classes is the distraction we cannot ignore. It isn't funny, it is extremely dangerous, and far too often public teachers are asked to grapple with it, not having been given any training or sense of

proportion. (See more in Chapter 11, "Fight Club.")
Verdict: *Do* something.

The Darkest Days

On day one of this attempt at memoir, I awoke thinking that this account must start with the worst day you could have teaching. I want to get it out there, get it over with, because it is bad, and will help to keep the rest of this accounting in its proper perspective. Because there is no denying the gravity of the trust put in the public educator. We are legally *in loco parentis*, signifying our legal responsibilities as parents while students are in our classrooms. I shudder to think of the weight of this responsibility, because when teachers take on that mantle, they may be morally compelled to stand between armed combatant children. They may be asked to place a very young person under citizen's arrest while protecting a potential victim of partner abuse. They may be mandated to report bruises to a child made by a parent with a wooden garden stake. There are too many stories like this that have happened to me. But the very worst was to read a small newspaper article about a murder victim found behind a dumpster in back of a local movie theater, and to feel my skin crawl with a premonition that the victim had been one of my students. Because it was.

Requiem for Two Sets of Brothers

Phuong Long was a large boy, in a school with Mexican-American and Vietnamese-American students comprising the majority. He was in a notably unruly class. He wasn't very disruptive in the class, in fact he was one of the few "good" ones, which meant he could sit in his seat longer than ten minutes and refrain from obnoxious interruption. I didn't get to know him well, since he seemed, by the standards in that class, to be an introvert. That's why I was quite surprised to see him hobbling in to my class the following year with a cast on his leg, using crutches.

Apparently he just wanted to visit, because all we did was chit-chat a little about how things were going for him: "Did you get the classes you needed?...Are you enjoying life?...Yes, I'm fine... Yes, the students this year *are* behaving better than your class last year." He laughed.

It was a typical conversation, but I probably had a curious look on my face. ("Is there something you need?") That was it. I found myself grinning that he had been kind enough to come by.

One week later, I was at a restaurant sitting across from my husband enjoying breakfast. He began to read me an article about a "man" whose body was found behind a dumpster behind a local movie theater, duct tape over his mouth. Unidentified as yet. My husband often remarked, "Hope it wasn't one of your students," when reading about various local crimes or misfortunes. But this time, *I* said it. Uncanny premonitions I had experienced in the past always felt like this. A calm dread.

Monday at lunch in the faculty lounge, a colleague sat alone. Out of the blue she started to tell me that a Yerba Buena student had been murdered over the weekend and found behind Gould's Cinema. His name was Phuong Long. "*Phuong Long*?!"

"Well now, there were two Phuong Long's."

"Well which one was this?!?"

"He was a very tall, large boy." I felt the acid rising in my throat.

"Did he have a cast on his leg?"

"Yes, that's how they identified him."

It made my soul explode from the inside. So alive—so dead. No in between. So young—so never. I remember her asking if I needed help, I must have been crying, I cannot remember. I went back to my classroom for the last period of the day, but I just couldn't focus. My whole being quaked. Somehow the office had already sent a substitute.

I will never forget her cold remark. She was a student advisor, pulled out of her office to relieve me. "We just have to get used to these things."

I'm a rebel. I will *never* get used to these things. The next day, I took my Teach for America friend with me, and we went to visit the family. Phuong 's sister was in her class, and we wanted to reach out and show our support. There was a good possibility that the killing was gang-related, since we had heard his mouth had been taped, which was a message for those involved that snitching was a capital offense. We wanted to show that his life was important to us, even if he had been involved with bad acts.

We were sorry we went. I have never in my life seen such unmitigated grief. The father kept wailing and putting his hands up to his face, the mother sat in stony silence, the rawness of their grief worse than skin sliced with razors. London, my dear friend, conferred with the sister quietly while I said over and over the only words I hoped would penetrate their obvious distress.

"He was my student. He was a good boy."

How *miniscule* the comfort I had to offer! I felt foolish and angry with myself for intruding. It came out the next day that Phuong 's own brother had done this irreversible, horrible act. How could the family ever find peace? Two boys lost forever. I went home and went to bed, ill, for two weeks. When I woke up each morning, I saw that face, Phuong 's face, alive and swimming up towards my consciousness. The darkest days.

A few years later, I would discover that teaching had more pain than one could be reasonably asked to bear. Yet bear it we must, and if we are to carry on, find a way to honor life in the presence of death. The survivors around us are so young, we must muster our courage as teachers to try to help them grapple with the unthinkable. Yet in truth we are no more able to grapple with it than they are.

I have had sets of twins in class before. Sometimes they're in the same class. Sometimes they're in different classes, and as it's so tempting for them, they make you feel funny in the first week of school as you say, "Didn't I just see you earlier today?" If they don't admit it, you might go on confused for a while. One day everyone is laughing at you as you discover they are identical. In this case, I only had one of the twins in my class. A very personable Vietnamese boy who sat in the middle of the room, surrounded by Black and Mexican students as well as other Vietnamese and Filipino students, a typical class at Yerba Buena High School.

His name began with a T, as did his brother's. He was shot and killed by a gang. All the students were telling me he hadn't been in the gang, but his brother had been hanging out with some bangers. It was a case of mistaken identity.

There was an empty desk in the middle of the room. We began to talk. Penny told me she had lived next door to them since they were little. The brother was taking it extremely hard. He told her he had slept in that room with their bunk beds their whole lives. And now his matching person was gone. He reported waking up seeing his brother there, silvery, ghostly. Several other students recounted stories of the boys. We grieved together. I kept a folder of his essays and gave them to his twin.

The school did not provide a memorial service for the boy as they had for others. Their rationale: it was gang-related. I will never forgive them for that one. Darkest days.

Now, the worst is over. If you learn to drive a manual transmission first, automatic will be a cinch. If you want to read more stories, they won't be this bad. Promise.

Comic Relief

I think there are four classes that vie for the prize of worst class I ever had. Classes in English One have been truly awful. I often tell about it because it was so funny, even though the students were terrible. I could have been fired and lost my credential because of what I did to that class.

The class was what we called an English One Repeater Class, because all of the students had attended or been assigned to English One as freshmen or even as sophomores but had failed and needed the English credit. They were now juniors and seniors in a "freshman" English class. I must say I enjoyed job security because the only class every student has to take all four years is English.

This particular class was sixth period, the last period of the day. Believe me, as a teacher, you are tired by then. Into the class walk thirty kids, none of whom can read or write on grade level, all of whom are feeling their second wind. Lunch has digested, and they are ready for action. You are ready for your nap. You get out the big, trusty, orange textbook, and try to have some reading and writing going on. But there is a different swirl of activity gathering around you, and it is bigger than you are. It is louder, and it starts to gain momentum. Wow, there are some big kids in here. There are six boys who weigh near 300 pounds and are over six feet tall, none of whom can read very well. When they are all on the same side of the room, the floor starts to tilt in that direction.

They may decide they would rather just have a huge discussion about sports or general goofiness, with the girls chiming in about he said/she said. Your calls to attention go completely unheeded. As though you weren't even there. *Exactly* as though you weren't even there, to the degree that there is no censorship on their topics or their choice of vocabulary.

"You know you have a bad class when the girls are talking about their bloody tampons out loud." How many times have we teachers shared this little tidbit of teacher inside information. If we survived first-year teaching, we feel we are veterans of some strange war between beings like "us," who were mostly really good students who liked to learn, and "them," the ones who are caged and restless, waiting for someone to make fun of, something to recount that will bring attention, someone to listen to their lives, someone to make the time go by faster until freedom at three o'clock.

This class was particularly rowdy. So much so, that the career technician in the next room used to look in curiously to see what all the hubbub was about—believe me, I didn't know. I was just trying to get through some stories in the book and get some meaningful writing going on, and perhaps a few lessons in grammar and usage. The students were expected to write five paragraph essays by the end of the year, on given topics. Good luck with that.

So, I yelled. I yelled a lot.

I yelled every day.I made them sit in a circle and read out loud to each other. We read some good stories and even better novels. They were all at about a sixth or seventh grade reading level, but we got through them. I insulted their actions. I told them they were driving me crazy. I told them they behaved like *animalitos* (little animals). I put disruptive kids outside in a little area that had lockers on each side and a chain link fence with a big gate. I locked the gate. This left a little concrete area about seven feet square for them to act up in. Seriously, I should have been fired for that. It was illegal. (There was another door to the outside in case of fire, just in case you are worrying about that.) I told them they could just go out there and act like *animalitos* all they wanted. I went to the door to see them rearing up like horses, and *whinny*ing!

They were sweet kids, and I loved them. I insulted their *behavior* every single day, yelled at them every single day, but made them read and write. And for some reason, they consistently told me I was their favorite teacher.

So, I tried an experiment. I told the career tech next door that I wanted to make a bet. I said, "You know that sixth period class?

How much do you wanna bet I can make them sit down at the beginning of every class for a week, fold their hands on their desks, and say, 'Good afternoon, Mrs. Demerson.'?" I told the tech that I would *not* bet money, and he said he would provide donuts for everyone if I won the bet. But he did not believe I could do it. Every day for a week, the tech looked in the window to my class at the beginning of sixth period. And every day for a week, they sat in a circle, folded their hands, and said, "Good afternoon, Mrs. Demerson."

Career tech had to pay up. I told the students I had won a bet.

They said, "You used us? We should get the money."

To their delight, I explained they were getting donuts instead.

How did I do it? I took the students one at a time out into the corral. I simply looked into their eyes and said, "Do you trust me?"

Without exception, one by one, they all said," Yes."

Then I explained what I wanted them to do. "Do you think you could do that? Will you do that for me?"

"Yes."

Sixth period, if you are out there, it was a sweet donut victory. Thank you for being you.

Have you ever hit a kid with a rolled-up newspaper? You know by now I am going to confess. Same class, last period of last day before Christmas break. Of course, we teachers expect a little folderol. But on this day, it was epic. I knew this class well enough to know that you don't reward them for all the jobs not done, nor do you offer them a party because they have made your class into a party every single chance they've had. But the other classes had parties, and there were goodies still uneaten on the tables in the back of the room. I had obtained permission from the other classes to let sixth period eat the leftovers.

Sixth period students arrived grumbling, knowing I had

specifically said they could *not* have a party. I informed them that they were welcome to the food in the back of the room. *Holy Jesus!* Thundering hooves! The room was literally shaking as they flew to the back, knocking over desks and anything else in the way. Food went flying across the room. By the time two-liter bottles of soda started to fly from New York to California, I jumped into action, grabbing newspapers, rolling them into a three-foot-long tube, and *Swat! Swat! Swat!* Calm *Down!* Sit *Down! Stop It!*

Order was restored, and a good time was had by all. *Joyeux Noel.* Don't judge.

The Thing About TV and Movie Teachers

The thing about TV and movie teachers is that they all have only one class. In public school, teachers often teach five and sometimes up to seven classes per day. In California, they often have thirty to thirty-five students in each class. That means at least one hundred and fifty students, who just keep coming in waves. I still have dreams about the sheer numbers of students with whom one needs to interact and create learning space. They all have their own minds, too! I remember my first days in teaching my own real classes for a full day. I was aghast at how they just kept coming. There is no chance to really get to know these students and very little time to assess individual learning needs. Test scores, in many cases, are woefully inadequate to tell us how to reach the individual. Discipline requires way too much of the class period; attention to errant behavior requires not just time but psychic energy and application of a particular type of intelligence.

It is said that teachers use eight areas of intelligence within the first ten minutes of class. These areas are found in different areas of the brain. No wonder we feel as though our brain activity has gone haywire. My husband, while considering a career shift to become a teacher, came to my class to practice teach with me for five weeks. He only worked with two classes, and after a few days reported that he had planned to go to the gym afterwards but had gone home to take a nap instead. Our daughter was substitute teaching in the same school—she said, "Dad, are you sure you want to do this? Have you ever seen Mom able to relax at brunch or lunch without some kid bugging her?"

"It's exhausting. I don't know how you do it!"

I don't either.

On TV, the teacher gets to get all up in the lives of her students. Notable movies like *Stand and Deliver* and *Freedom Writers* are inspirational. But that's because those teachers became monks to the cause—threw themselves in to their work. Other areas suffered. Sadly, both Jaime Escalante and Erin Gruwellvie got divorced. Erin left teaching after three years. We were warned in teacher training to beware of too much immersion making one into a nun. But no one could prepare me for how much I would want to be a hero. I have dreams that the Columbine-type assassins come to my school, but I use my Kung Fu and quick thinking to foil their plot and save the students. Catcher in the Rye syndrome. It ain't gonna happen. We can't save them all, even if we do sacrifice ourselves. And then what would be left to give?

Chapter 2. Autism

My memories of students with autism are coming to the forefront now because my husband and I have been enjoying a 2010 TV series called *Parenthood*, in which a boy with autism is one of the main characters, and another adult realizes he is autistic as well. It brings to mind all the really, really bad portrayals of this syndrome that have been shown. *The Big Bang* and *Bones* have had characters that demonstrate similar character traits, but the portrayals do not ring true. To me it isn't really funny, and it isn't really charming. We aren't doing any students, parents, or teachers any favors by putting these images out there. A new, somewhat more realistic portrayal has emerged with a program called *The Good Doctor*. It gives me hope that more understanding will ensue. Reading the book *Funny, You Don't Look Autistic,* by Michael McCreary, is another way to appreciate the nuances of the spectrum. And as I finish this account, the new series *As We See It* is airing, with autistic actors. My autistic friends are excited, and it is being well-received. My husband and I love the show, and hope it returns for a second season.

Autism is so often misunderstood, misdiagnosed, undiagnosed. Sometimes kids are just a bit nerdy, and so are their teachers. When a teacher in public school gets a roll sheet, the saying goes, "You got who you got." Unless you are in with the in crowd like some people I know—for whom doors magically open and difficult students are magically removed from their rolls—you will have to manage a classroom with random students that the administration has put in your class. They may be placed

in what the jargon of Special Education would
restrictive environment." This means they will ᴜ y ₋ ₋
student with a special learning need into a class or situation
where he or she is most motivated and potentially able to fit in
socially. That leaves a lot of room for error.

The rest of the students and the attitude of the teacher play a
huge role in whether the environment is freeing or creates more
restrictions. If interaction between the student and classmates
is not managed by the teacher, misunderstandings will occur.
Too often students may bully them; teachers may neglect
them. Another danger is spoiling the more appealing students
because we feel sorry for them and don't raise our expectations
enough. With students with autism, we often think it has been
successful "mainstreaming," when the student behavior is calm
enough that they don't rock the boat. But has learning taken
place? Has the student reached potential for social growth? Very
difficult to say.

Vinh Ngo was one such student. The challenge of having him
in class must be measured against the challenge he faced
each day when he wakes up and faces life in his own brain.
The first time I noticed that Vinh had specific problems was
when he answered questions with esoteric responses that the
typical sixteen-year-old would not know or ever volunteer in
that setting. An overabundance of knowledge in a very specific
isolated topic is one of the manifestations of this syndrome. It
doesn't mean a kid is autistic just because he knows *all* about air
flight trajectories; the signal is when he can't seem to turn off
the flow of talk about the topic when others have moved on. The
signature manifestation of this syndrome is the inability to read
social cues that others of the same age group have learned to
understand and respond to appropriately.

Knowing autistic kids helped me learn so much. I learned to
discipline myself to be more aware of student reactions. And I
learned to breathe and take time with each situation: time to

ιssess and empathize, time to process what is really happening with interactions. But it takes an experienced teacher to have the confidence to let the class simmer a bit as we figure out how we balance these concerns. When we worry about other bad behavior surfacing as we take stock of a situation with a small group, we risk losing control of the larger group. This takes practice and eyes in the back of the head.

We take so much for granted when we gather socially. For a kid to know when to stop talking about radiation or dinosaurs or electricity seems like something we learned by third grade, so by fourth grade, this inability may be diagnosed as autism. Unfortunately, many kids go undiagnosed into adulthood and struggle with their neurodivergence unaided.

Vinh attacked another student. He started trying to stab the boy with a pen. The other students had all told me not to seat Vinh in a certain place, that there would be a problem. But there are only so many seating arrangements one can make before the class groupings just don't work. Vinh pretty much needed to be moved away from everybody because of his inappropriate comments and his annoying mannerisms.

The day he tried to stab the other kid; I honestly didn't want to deal with it. I knew the other students bothered him more than he bothered them. I knew the kid other probably deserved to have Vinh retaliate, but somebody had to be the adult in the room. Alas, I had to be the one to figure out what was really going on and restore a learning environment. So I told Vinh to go into the computer lab next door and sit where I could see him through the window. I asked the other boy to step outside the other door. Vinh was extremely agitated, spitting while he talked, tightly gripping his backpack, and saying over and over, "He stole my red pen." Wow. How to understand such a violent over-reaction to a missing pen. Why was that so upsetting?

"Can I get you another pen?"

"*No*! That was my pen! I left it on the table in my class and he was the only one who could have taken it!"

"Do you think you can calm down enough to sit here and play a video game, while I talk to [the other boy]?"

"OK."

The other boy stated unequivocally that he did not take Vinh's pen, and that he had one just like it because they were required in that class. He seemed very calm, willing to forget about it and resume classroom activity. But that was the conundrum: what to do about Vinh. He had assaulted another student, but clearly his condition was responsible for his inability to manage a perceived injustice. There had been too many times when he was taken advantage of, made fun of, lied to, told to shut up. Anger actually was the appropriate response. But how to roll it back and manage aggression was a problem too large for Vinh that day. I considered it a victory that he didn't draw blood or store up his animosity for a later explosion. He played a violent video game instead. I called his next period teacher and explained that Vinh may not show up, and that I would be happy to help him catch up on anything he missed. The teacher informed me that he'd had the same problem with Vinh the previous year. A clear picture was emerging of a boy with few coping skills.

One by one, again, I took each of the students outside, looked in their eyes, and told them: "If I were to tell you that someone in our class has a condition, let's say cancer, would you be willing to give that kid a break and be especially careful with how you treat him? If, for example, he needed help carrying something or getting lunch?"

"Yes, Mrs. Demerson."

"Well, I am going to tell you that someone in our class does have a condition that makes it *very* difficult to interact well with others. It is something that causes that person an awful lot of pain every single day of his life. Would you be willing to just let that person alone, ignore his inappropriate comments, and let me deal with him?"

"Yes, of course, Mrs. Demerson."

"I think by now you may know who I am talking about, so just remember how very painful life can be when stuck with this problem."

Vinh had a peaceful year in my class after that. He came back to grace my room with his thousand answers to technical subjects the following year—he was my aide. An aide with high intelligence and a fast learning curve who doesn't mind being glued to a computer is an aide I would pay money for (and did, when they would work after school). Vinh obviously liked me, but he would say gauche things to me all the time.

Once two students were playing music and chatting with me at lunch. We got on to the subject of how funny my mom was when she was in early stages of Alzheimer's and put her slippers in the microwave. She used to do that when her feet were cold (always) when we had had a regular oven, so it didn't seem illogical. But the slippers caught on fire! But that wasn't the funny part, I explained, the funny part was: she did it again! This time the assisted care facility made her give up her studio apartment and move to a nursing care room. I was laughing hard at this and so were the girls because it was endearing and inevitable. Then a few moments later I was musing, "She actually passed away a year or so later. I really miss her."

Vinh picked this moment to start laughing. "*No, Vinh.* That's not the funny part."

The girls were aghast. But they didn't really understand that Asperger's makes a mess out of what are already complicated social interactions. One cue misread can cause a huge gaffe. What a minefield for Vinh to navigate! The beauty of the story is that the girls understood completely that *they* were not to laugh at *Vinh.* They had that innate facility that helped them read my extremely subtle cues.

The next Christmas season, I sent Vinh a video game that he had been wanting. He was really surprised by that. He kept asking me what I wanted for Christmas, and I kept telling him I wanted a card, nothing more, and that would mean more to me than anything. But he persisted. One day he heard me saying how much I loved gel pens. He kept asking me, "So, you really like gel pens?" over and over. I think by now I had figured out who was getting some gel pens for Christmas. (*Me!* I love school supplies!) Vinh brought me a pack of old, partially used gel pens. No wrapping paper, no card. They were odd, but significant. I appreciated the attempt, and told him over and over, "Thank you for the thoughtful gift." I once asked Vinh if his parents had ever had him tested. His answers led me to believe he had no clue of his syndrome. But the manifestations were so very clear.

And life for him won't be "no crystal stair,"[i]

When you get kids with autism, their inappropriate behavior can be quite shocking. A typical behavior is over-answering. I have had to tell several students that they must give other students a chance to respond, no matter how difficult it may be to wait when you already know. Other students tend to get really annoyed at this, and even when they are subtle, don't think that the autistic student doesn't see the eye-rolling and hear the whispers. A teacher's challenge is to stay impassive and try, calmly, to divert the student to another pursuit. Much more easily said than done.

A somewhat less typical but far more upsetting behavior is self-consoling, which may be in the form of masturbation. When you see students rubbing themselves, the tendency is to panic. It must be stopped before other students see, and parents must be informed. How awkward is that! I had a set of twins, brothers, one of whom dragged his suitcase of schoolbooks around with him, on a campus where every single other student used a backpack. The other rubbed his crotch in class and made a comment out loud after every, single, thing I said.

These are the stories of the real classrooms of America. And you wonder why we need tenure? If we don't have at least a couple of years to figure out how to grapple with these very real situations, we cannot master our craft. We need the security to try new things, and we will make mistakes along the way. Public school teachers care for the young in our society, and at our best, we take on all comers with flexibility and a willingness to adapt to the most intricate social configurations. And then there's the lesson plan.

Chapter 3. Learning Gap

This morning one of my former students reposted a little chart on Facebook that reads:

Things I Never Learned in High School
How to do taxes
What taxes are
How to vote
How to write a resume/cover letter
Anything to do with banking
How to apply for loans for college
How to buy a car or house... but thank my Lucky Stars, I can tell you all about Pythagorean Theorems

To which someone commented: There is only one Pythagorean Theorem, ya dong.

Perhaps many of us wish we had learned more relevant material in high school. One of the principles I learned in Montessori teacher training is that learning should be holistic, and project-centered. The Demerson Theorem is that if we had followed that precept, real-world study projects should incorporate all of the areas of study. Paolo Freire[ii] suggested that urgent, real-world projects engage their learning at unprecedented levels.

I taught English in fifty-minute slices. I felt fortunate to do so, because in English class, one can use literature to open discourse about any topic whatsoever. When teaching the novel *Beloved*, by Toni Morrison, I found that many students, even girls, did not even know that their menstrual cycle was twenty-eight days. This is significant on so many levels. I have often thought about how we must re-teach spelling and capitalization every year. Why aren't we re-teaching the basic facts of our own bodies? My students came to school approximately 19,000 hours before graduating from high school. Yet they remained woefully ignorant of so much of life's most critical information.

Some of the best lessons in my classes have happened when someone asked a question that seemed to have nothing to do with the topic at hand. If someone asked for help, for example, on a college application, we could put it on the overhead projector, and show the whole class the process. If we had a math question that students could not solve, we could put it on the whiteboard and have someone help us solve it. (So many math problems come down to knowing vocabulary.) English teachers often find out in March just how disparate the classes are these kids are taking when standardized tests are put in front of junior students. From "Integrated Science" to physics, these kids may be taking anywhere from a remedial level to an advanced (AP) level. They are given different tests depending on the math, science, and social science classes they are in. Yet every junior-year student is expected to test on the same English skills. The test often begins with a passage from Nathaniel Hawthorne, whose colonial American style and vocabulary requires advanced study even among English teachers. Just what are we trying to find out about our students? We continue to try to find out what they do *not* know, instead of giving them the opportunity to show us what they *do* know.

High school teachers are required to be subject-matter experts. Yet many of my student teachers managed to have achieved university degrees in English and were undereducated in grammar. They then taught classes of immigrant students who were often below grade level in their home language, and who were now confronted with English—one of the most perplexing languages ever evolved, with almost as many exceptions to the rules as there are rules. Sometimes I wonder about that misfit. If I am not comfortable with the grammar of my own language, how do I begin to share the exciting knowledge with a new English learner? My best friend who is a brilliant Spanish and English as a second language teacher encourages me to let it go. She teases me unmercifully about my strict grammar, and once at dinner asked everyone to use the *non*-word "multi-tasking" over and over until I was starting to feel picked on! "Task" is not an intransitive verb. I stand firm even when dictionaries change! You'll never get me to be happy with "irregardless."

In 1991-1995, I taught at Foothill High School. It had previously been a "continuation school," a school for students who had been kicked out of four or five of the other high schools in the district. The district, in all its wisdom, had shut down the continuation school, ostensibly because there was so much strife among the staff. Then someone noticed that they had forgotten about the pregnant and parenting girls whose day care center would still be housed on campus. Consequently, they still needed classes on campus. So they hired me to teach the girls all of their subjects on independent study contracts in a self-contained classroom environment. Our district of eleven high schools had forty parents, forty pregnant girls, and *eighty* girls on the waiting list at any given time. (Pause for horror.)

I had found out early that teen childbearing could be a huge obstacle to graduation rates. When I began teaching in the district in 1984, *one third* of the freshman girls in my high school would not graduate due to a pregnancy. This number was staggering. One girl in my freshman class was pregnant at fourteen. Her best friend decided to get pregnant too, so they could raise their babies at the same time! The first girl confided in me that she had recently discovered a sad fact: her father was her grandfather. Her mother was the victim of incest and forced to be a teen mom herself.

As that was my very first real high school class on my own, I must say it was a quick education for me. I loved those two girls, despite their odd views of parenting. I remember the first pregnant girl's name was Jasmine, and she had a way of looking at me that was at once both sly and innocent. As a teacher, I rarely involve myself in individual family politics, because to disparage a parent is to disparage the child. Most of us feel we can complain about our family members, but don't let anyone else do it! This is the inherent understanding underlying the "Yo Momma" jokes, and why they are so universally understood to be insulting, funny only when told in a certain way. *We* cannot tell a student her mom was dumb to have her so young. We cannot possibly know the circumstances.

Despite my aversion to the idea of a teen parent, I did feel that once the decision had been made to bring a baby into the world, we must give our very best to see that the mother is well-educated and the child healthy and in a stable environment. When I went back to teach in a comprehensive school, I still maintained the habit of providing a little shower for any expectant mother, with her friends, a cake, and some presents —I always provided books for the baby. I told the girl and her friends about the importance of reading to the baby and made it clear that I expected to check back in with them later to make sure they were reading together. I might see a young mother with her child at the mall, and she'd better expect to be drilled on their reading experiences!

The childcare center at Foothill High School offered the girls breakfast and lunch for them and their babies, a free school bus ride from their home school to the continuation campus, a free ride home, childcare, and parenting classes. A nurse-midwife was there for health instruction. They even provided taxi rides to the local high school for advanced classes that we could not offer. While this program seemed ideal if we were to support our low-income community, there were some problems with it.

Why not have another baby now, while everything is free?

More Learning Gap

How is it that a girl gets pregnant in the AIDS generation? Clearly, she had unprotected sex. How was the threat of AIDS, once a death sentence, not enough of a deterrent to unprotected sex? (In schools where I had worked before, folks were aware of the statistic that on-site condom-dispensing at school was the only strategy that decreased teen pregnancy. But the parents in the community would not permit it.)

The answers are many and varied. In the heat of the moment we all make mistakes. Sometimes we are victims of statutory or outright rape. But most often girls are victims of the saddening belief that the boyfriend is the knight in shining armor who will take them away from their unsatisfactory life, to play house with their baby into the happily ever after.

Or as my husband had once pointed out when he heard my vitriolic rant about teen pregnancy, "How do you know what it feels like to come from the ghetto and know you are trapped and will never get out? And feel like you just want a small person to look up to you and love you and be your companion through all the shit!"

That was Zen enlightenment for me.

I was shocked that statistics were not taught. They weren't apprised about family life and how unlikely it would be that a couple from high school would stay together. These ideas were not only not taught, but even when taught, they were not believed. Many of my girls thought that sex was the way you show love, and they were desperate for that loving touch.

Many of them were daughters of mothers who had been teens themselves when they were born, yet they did not see the irony that they would pre-destine their children to the same under-educated, under-provided state. The cycle of teen pregnancy perpetuates poverty. Studies are clear that the educational level of the child closely correlates to the educational level of its *mother*. And as for the myth that the girls were sex fiends or promiscuous, sadly most of the girls who had had a baby, had never had an orgasm. To suffer all of the consequences but have experienced very little of the joy or understanding of the effect of sexuality in their lives was the plight of my teenage parenting students.

I would tear at my hair every single time a girl would write an essay explaining that she was pregnant and could not *spell pregnant!* One girl, who was learning disabled, had two children already and was about to have a third at the age of fifteen. She told me that she would never be good at anything, but she knew she could be a good mom. Sadly, her babies were often ill, the result of her inattention to health precautions. She wasn't a good hand-washer, and the aides had trouble helping her to understand the connection between hygiene and the exchange of germs from the day care center.

The learning skills of the students varied widely. On the other end of the spectrum, one girl stands out in my memory because she was one of the few who was to qualify for a four-year college out of high school. She was nineteen. She had the most parental support, and the father of her babies married her. As she was about to have twins, she was put on bed rest toward the end of the pregnancy. The district provided for home schooling, so I went to her home once a week with her lessons, and she graduated on time with her class, with two little babies in tow.

I have attended many emotional graduations, but the ones that touched me the most were the ones where young women somehow made it through having a baby, and still managing to graduate on time.

When I was teaching all the subjects myself and the childcare teachers were tracking the progress of the students into their chosen post-secondary pursuits, we graduated one hundred percent of the seniors.

One hundred percent.

I used a system that was simplified and provided immediate visual feedback by way of my big, red initials after every listed task was completed. Every girl was cajoled, supported, harassed, tutored, and forced to get her credits. I sent my aide to the home of a girl who needed to pass only one more test. She spent the night with the girl, and they stayed up all night studying. The next morning, she was there bright and early, passed her test, and graduated in the afternoon!

My aide was a teen mom herself, and told those girls, "If I can do it, so can you. I don't get a free bus ride, but don't you see me here every day, after I've dropped off my baby girl and taken the public bus across town to get here on time?"

This was more motivational than anything I could possibly have said. Most importantly, almost every one of those girls went on to post-secondary education. And *none* of them had a second baby while in school. The statistics of the school before I arrived showed that many were having that second pregnancy, and far fewer were graduating and going on to college.

One girl, Brianna, surprised me by recognizing my daughter when she came by after school. It turns out she had lived across from us when my girls were little. They had been playmates. Here she was in high school, with a little baby.

Her baby's father was an MP Hood, a gang so named because its members lived near Mount Pleasant High School. To my horror, many girls dressed their little babies in red or blue (rival gang) bandanas, the emblems of the local branch of the "Bloods" or "Crips" or *"Norteño"* or *"Sureño"* gangs. Bringing gang life to a new generation.

One day as Brianna was standing on a street corner, her baby's father, seeing her with the baby in her arms standing across the street from him, raised his gun and fired at her. Thank god the bullet missed her and the baby. We counseled her to leave the area for good—if she cared about her baby and herself at all. The last I heard she had moved to a neighboring state, and I was relieved to hear it. Drastic times call for drastic measures.

What could have been going through her mind to choose this psychotic troublemaker to father her baby? Brianna cared about my opinion of her, and I like to think I helped to save her life (and perhaps her baby's). *Catcher in the Rye* syndrome again. It was a team effort, because the teachers in the childcare center also kept a watchful eye for our young ladies. Their input was invaluable as they not only cared for the little ones, but they also taught their mamas (and some teen fathers as well). Joyce Taylor, Pat Bonasera, and Mary Jacobs, there is a special place for you in my heart, as I know there are children out there now in their twenties who owe their good starts to you.

One girl was pregnant at twelve years old. (Our district had a portable classroom at one of the middle schools, for the pregnant tweenies.) Her mother's boyfriend had raped her. Her older sister was in our school, having had her baby the year before. I met the mother, and by her appearance, she looked as though she were their sister instead of their mom, wearing more makeup and a short, tight skirt. I could simply not believe that she had not seen to it that the twelve-year-old have a termination. Preserving the baby at the risk of the mother was a travesty. Asking her little body to stretch to those limits was so dangerous.

The twelve-year-old survived labor and ran away to Mexico. She said that every time she looked at her child, she saw her rapist. Her teenage sister was angry with her and said, "If you don't want her, give her to me!" It is very, very hard to see how that would have been the solution. The poor girl came back eventually. When I met her, I was struck with her big, beautiful eyes, and wanted to get her a teddy bear. To think she had gone through rape, pregnancy, and labor made me want to scream. I wanted to choke the mom. I wanted to bludgeon the rapist. I never found out if he had been prosecuted.

I found it extremely difficult to maintain an objective point of view. Sometimes I would read that the current social message was that these girls had low self-esteem. While I found that to be the case in many instances, I also found the problem to be *high* self-esteem. Many girls felt that they had the right to have that baby because they could raise it just fine. They couldn't see why anyone wouldn't want to help them. One girl actually complained, "My mom will babysit for me while I'm at work or at school, but *she won't babysit for me to go out!*"

"Really?" I asked her point blank, "Did you hear what you just said? Your mom did *not* have this baby. She already had her babies!"

The pain of watching these girls and their families go through hell was too much for me. I seemed to have a sign on my forehead that said, "Tell me your worst problem." And every brunch or lunch, after school, and sometimes during class if it were too urgent to postpone, some hapless young lady would do just that.

The stories were so ineffably sad.

One day I was in my classroom and my best friend, the glorious Kim Evans, was paying a visit from across the campus, where she taught in the Welcome Center program for new immigrant students. A parenting student was telling me about how her baby's father's mom had been taking care of her baby, but she was a little concerned about that because the woman was a crack addict. I responded calmly, telling her that I was glad she was thinking carefully about this, and asking her if there were someone else who could possibly do the babysitting. I acted as though it were an everyday question! Kim, my teacher "bestie," was in abject horror—it was all she could do to keep from screaming out, "*Oh My God!*" But I knew that if I would be able to convince the girl that I believed in her competence to grapple with the problem, she would rise to the occasion and do the right thing. Judging and yelling don't always work with adolescents. She made the right choice and removed the baby from the crackhead's care.

Kim now recites this anecdote as evidence of my skill with troubled youth, but I took it for granted that it's important to remain calm when the world we thought we knew is turned on its ear. In fact, if ever there is a time to remain calm, it is when a teenager is in crisis. They have enough hormonal insanity for all of us; we don't need to stir it further.

The students in the program and I read together Maya Angelou's *I Know Why the Caged Bird Sings.* The girls wrote a curriculum for the book in which they created critical thinking questions that ran the gamut of *Bloom's Taxonomy.*[iii] They learned to ask probing questions while engaging with one of the most beloved memoirs of all time. When we got to the end, when the girls find out Angelou had a baby at seventeen, they were so motivated to read more.

The same year, *The Joy Luck Club* came out in the theater. We planned a field trip and took the girls to see the movie. Their reactions varied, but none were untouched by the stories of mothers and daughters. We teachers sat in silence and watched the group. As the part about the mother whose baby drowned in the bath filled the screen, we were surprised to hear some crying, but also some laughter. As we talked about it later, we realized the pressure was just too much for them to internalize. The girls who had been laughing were doing so as a release mechanism. Too sad and horrified to cry, their only defense was to burst out laughing. As the childcare teachers and I came to this realization, we were very glad that we had exposed them to such an artistic expression of pathos and impact.

When asked by a wonderful principal what I wanted for my students, I asked her for ethnic novels, and placed *The Joy Luck Club* very high on the list. She remembered a year later, when the *San José Mercury News* asked her what we needed at the school. I was so delighted that the little Post-it upon which this principal had written my wish list had been placed in her bra (she kept her reminders in there), and it had placed a stamp on her heart. My books arrived, and a new set of students would read and see the enlightening story. That principal and I started a profound friendship after sharing the experience of working at this unique school. When my own mom passed away during the course of that year, Alicia Mendeke became my Lady of Light.

Worst story. One young lady was pregnant with her second baby by a father who was a con man, very irresponsible. The young lady had only been a freshman when she got pregnant the first time; the second time was probably an accident because the boyfriend had only come out of jail long enough to impregnate her; then he was sent back for another crime. She was a quiet girl whose grades reflected evidence of a mind at work.

I was so sad to hear that her second baby died of SIDS (sudden infant death syndrome.) We teachers went to support our student. The jail let the father out to go to the funeral, and I saw him at the gravesite as everyone was leaving. I hesitated to leave, because somehow, I knew that he was about to do something crazy. As I watched in horror, he threw himself into the open grave, wailing and pounding his fists into the earth. I approached and with tears flowing, told him, *"You gotta get up. You have to get up for your son."* He somehow managed to rise, just as the guards came to cuff him and take him back. That is a sight I would not wish on anyone. It haunts me still. I don't think his children's mother saw, and I never saw any of them again. Teen fathers suffer, too.

Need more comic relief? While the girls were in a program with only girls, we talked about everything with a candor that was very refreshing. At the time, my mom was in a nursing home near my house, and Alzheimer's required that she have constant care. I had just bought her several pairs of granny panties, and had taken them out of the bag and was holding them up to the outside of my clothing, showing them off to the girls for a bit of a giggle, when in through the partition walked Mr. Smith, the visiting math teacher! Was my face red! One gets a bit too comfortable in the all-female environment, and apparently the poor guy was a bit flummoxed, because he popped back through to the other side. We all tried to stifle our giggles, and I waited for the heat to die down in my face. I wear embarrassment like a red flag, so by the time he resurfaced moments later, I was embarrassed that I was embarrassed! After all, we all have to wear underpants (well, pretty much all of us) ...

Once I had taken Mom to the local Eastridge Mall, entered arm in arm into Macy's, and noticed she was tugging my arm a bit, lagging a bit behind. I let go and waited for her to walk ahead of me. I glanced down towards her feet in time to notice her pulling her second foot out of a pair of silky underpanties! There they lay on the floor, as Mom kept her head up, and just kept walking! Bless the oblivion of age and mental incapacity, she just didn't care, so neither did I. Let's go, Mom!

When I initially took the position, the school was only for the girls and a special education classroom. They soon added a Welcome Center for pre-literate immigrant students. These schools within-a-school were functioning extremely well, but the district chose to change back to the former mode, a full continuation school. That meant that the boys would be back, the boys who had been kicked out of so many opportunities.

Although most of the parenting girls exhibited risky behavior even before becoming pregnant (one that I know of lost custody because her child ran into the street while she was inside her house getting high), most of them had *not* been problem students. I had a hard time seeing how being in a continuation school was the best placement for them. While we had the girls almost to themselves, they came to school wearing comfortable sweatsuits, and were in a room with all females, free to talk about anything and free from sexual pressures and temptations. As soon as boys came on campus, many girls went back to wearing revealing clothing and carrying themselves in a flirtatious manner, exhibiting behaviors that contributed to their situation in the first place. I heard from former teachers there that gangster boys who went there would sometimes ask their girlfriends to carry their guns in their purses for them! Apparently, they would be less likely to be searched. How could it be advisable to bring boys back on campus? I told the principal to let me know by March if they were going to change the format the following year, so I could put in my transfer by April. He did and I did.

Returning to a comprehensive high school made me realize right away just how strained I had become while listening to all of the stories of the young and the restless. I recommend that every teacher who works with this challenging type of population take some time out to work with a "regular" group. Then if you have a sign on your forehead that says "Tell me your worst nightmare," the students have many more adults in their environment wearing the same sign. Perhaps, as they did with me, only a few per semester will come in at lunch to do just that. Because you carry their sadness with you, and it hurts. It affects your own family life, and it affects your general outlook on life. When you start to think all teenagers have these serious, serious, heart-wrenching problems, you forget how many are usually cheerful and live in sane families who are supportive and loving. You forget that some teenagers do their homework and go to college.

You forget, most importantly of all, to give yourself a break and let go of the sense that you were somehow supposed to have done more to help. You didn't get them into their situations, and you cannot get them out. You can only listen, offer what wisdom your life has brought you, and give them a purposive academic project that can engage their minds and give them a sense of accomplishment. After all, nothing succeeds like success.

Chapter 4. Cheating and Using Your Class for Another Teacher's Work

When a student copies another student's work or plagiarizes, it is usually because of the learning gap. Think about this: if you are behind your peers in every single class, you might begin to take any shortcut you can get. If your parents are going to beat your butt or lose respect for you, you might feel the pressure is just too great to withstand the temptation to sneak that peek at another's paper. Teachers must show compassion and give learning opportunities.

I have had students get caught cheating so obviously that I couldn't believe they didn't even bother to shield their papers. They would have a math or social studies paper of another student side by side with theirs, copying just as fast as they could, oblivious to the lesson I was teaching. My strategy was to circulate to the offender's desk, slide the papers off and take them to my desk, where I would put them in a large envelope, address it to the teacher whose assignment the student was copying, and send it to his or her room with a note attached explaining what happened. But before sending it, I would offer this option quietly to the individual:

"You are about to have consequences for copying. Right now you have the opportunity to 'man up,' (or 'be a woman'), and go to the teacher yourself, explain that you did it, and explain why. There is also that other student involved. What are you going to tell that friend of yours who loaned you the paper? I will follow up on this because it is an opportunity to see how an adult can rectify a mistake by taking responsibility. You can be that adult. You choose. Because if you don't, I will. But if *you* do, I can almost guarantee your teacher will be willing to work with you to be able to do the work yourself. Because whom are you really cheating? Your teacher already *knows* how to do the work. You are cheating your own *brain* because you are not giving it the opportunity to build itself from within. You will be happier and more deeply satisfied if you can do this work yourself. And if you get caught cheating on one of *my* tests, I will give you a zero on the test and notify the office that you are to be suspended."

The key is the follow-up. Give the teacher the respect he or she deserves by a phone call or email. Offer your services to make time for the students to get the help they need. Bottom line, we are not trying to be police. We are trying to see that the hard work of learning gets done. Cheating isn't yet a character flaw set in stone; it's a mistake. Remember the potential for change?

One of my lovely students came in one day, crying because she had cheated her way through every single test she had taken in high school, including the California High School Exit Exam. I asked her how she did that, and she admitted that the "smart" kids were taking it first and passing the answers to others.

"Now," she said, "I'm scared to death I won't know a thing in college, and I'll flunk out."

I told her there was help for her and steered her in the right direction for support services. When I told this story at an English Department Chair meeting, I was disgusted with the punitive attitudes of some of the department chairpersons from other high schools. They were adamant that if it had been up to them, she would have been punished and failed. How would she learn from failure? What would she learn that her collapse had not already taught? That lovely girl is now furthering her education, faring exceptionally well, and enjoying what she learns. Isn't that the best outcome? When is it punishment for edification of the student, and when is it merely our desire to prove our power over these young people, who are still works in progress? We must use our innate sense of the student's true motives, and respond on a case-by-case basis.

I repeat this to myself on a regular basis: "Education is an aid to life." – Dr. Maria Montessori

Chapter 5. Sadness

There is a difference between sadness and depression.

In the early eighties, I was learning my craft, teaching, and learning about the way the school operated. Apparently, there was a real "in crowd" mentality among staff at the school, which led me to believe that adults don't change much in social dynamics. I was in the "out crowd," and they surely didn't let me forget it. New teachers are often asked to become advisors of clubs or classes and sort of pay their dues in unpaid overtime, ostensibly getting to know the students from a broader perspective. I was recruited to be a freshman class advisor—not knowing what that would entail. I discovered that freshman advisors don't really advise. (One student said I would be a good advisor because, "You give good advices.") That being the case, I gave it a try.

It turns out that, sadly, all the classes do is compete against each other in "Spirit Week," a nod to the days when the homecoming football game used to be attended by the community. Students would set up rallies, before-school brunch, and lunchtime skits with lots of posters, balloons, and cheering. In the spring, they would create "Fantastics," another excuse for the classes to compete against each other with skits and games in the gym. I couldn't imagine anything more horrifying! The word advisor conjured up helping students plan their lives in some meaningful way. I talked it over with my husband, and he suggested something much closer to my heart. I quickly abdicated "Freshman Advisor."

This week while going through keepsakes box, I found an old

article from the high school paper of that week.

Hunger Project raises money, consciousness

The "Feed the World Project," begun just before Valentine's Day, has been a success, raising over $375 for Ethiopian famine relief and helping Overfelt students to become more aware of the crisis in Africa.

Through Valentine's messages sold at $1 apiece and contributions from the faculty and staff, the money was raised within a 10-day period.

Much of the success was due to the efforts of a few fine people. The generosity of the BSU, which matched the donations of its members, and a few concerned teachers like Ms. Charlene Mello, Ms. Theresa McRae, and Mr. Jim Atencio were invaluable. The work of Odyssey staffers Robert Burns, Judy Crowley, Irma Gonzales, Jon Gascon, and Blanca Martinez got the project off the ground.

Further, freshman adviser Ms. Hannah Demerson took the idea and went beyond our wildest expectations. She got a videotape of the NBC news reports on the Ethiopian famine, showed it to world cultures classes, and organized a freshman class paper drive. The response of students has now led her to form a club to help raise money for those starving in Africa and to be of service to the hungry here in the valley.

On almost all fronts, the "Feed the World Project" has been a tremendous success. Unfortunately, one inconsiderate person spoiled it for a couple of our students. By submitting a fake "message" in the Valentine's Day issue, he or she hurt innocent people. The Odyssey apologizes to Sonia Media for any embarrassment or inconvenience caused by the message.

Mr. Douglas Day,
Odyssey Adviser

There was a famine in Ethiopia of vast proportions. The British media picked it up first, and did an impressive job of covering the problem. I talked to the students about it, and we decided to form a club, The Feed the World Club. I can proudly say that we raised over $3,000 for famine relief with proceeds from a dance we sponsored, helped the local homeless and hungry by serving in soup kitchens once a week, organized food and blanket drives, and cleaned up the entire area around the perimeter of the school of its paper and detritus on several Saturdays.

The soup kitchen experience ranks high in the list of accomplishments of which I am most proud. Every week we went to either Loaves and Fishes or Martha's Kitchen to help prepare and serve meals for lines of homeless people in San José. At least five of us would go every time to serve, as we found ourselves flanked by mostly white students from private Catholic high schools who were required to do this as community service for graduation.

For us, it was a joy and an awakening. Many of my students,

while standing in line, would look up, and to their surprise, find themselves looking into the eyes of a kid they had known when they were younger. Our students were two paychecks away from the homeless line themselves, yet they were the most willing to help! I was so inspired by their activism. These were kids who came from every level of school achievement, from my honors students to the special education students, and all left a little changed by the experience. My own daughters were pre-school and elementary school-aged, and I brought them along for the experience. I remember how cute they looked watching and coloring or doing their homework on the little benches, too young to be allowed to help much, as we rolled up our sleeves and chopped vegetables, bussed tables, and served in the line.

Later, Rainy would write about the experience that she read aloud in a tribute to me (see Foreword) at my retirement dinner, which she and our other daughter, Spirit, planned. It made me cry to hear that she had been touched by seeing children her age hungry and so willing to accept the toys we would bring for them.

We could eat a meal as well, and many times we did, side by side with the needy and unwashed. It was a clear education for us that at *least* two-thirds of the homeless were clearly mentally ill and would be unable to hold a job even if one were available. One lady I remember kept her fingers clenched on both hands with a Bic plastic disposable cigarette lighter in between each two fingers, eight lighters in all. Her hair was kept shaved in a buzz cut. She would crouch in corners of the room, always in a heavy coat, eyes peering out of hooded lids with a suspicious glare. She looked like the embodiment of madness. Who knows what her life might have been like before mental illness? The priest told us she had been a professor at Berkeley before her life took this turn. It was a window into what could happen to any of us, and it provided us with both gratitude for whatever sanity we might cling to, and compassion for those whose grip had slipped.

My resentment for those who closed so many opportunities for the homeless was carried forward from my days working in the state mental hospital in Southern California. It was Ronald Reagan who closed facilities and made no provision for those left literally out in the cold. I believed in teaching these lessons to the young, and what began as a wrong turn for me to become freshman class advisor turned into one of the best of all teaching opportunities. We were sad for the people we served but helping enlightened us and lightened our hearts.

The difference between sadness and depression is action.

Bread and Guns

I like to say that I've only taken a gun away from a student once. That way everyone can think my life as a teacher in East San José was daring, and that I was brave and a little bit funny. At San José's teacher college, I told my fellow teacher trainees that I would be teaching at Overfelt at the end of the credentialing program. They warned me that the girls on the volleyball team I was about to coach carried blades in their gym bags when they went to play at other schools. I wondered if it were true—oooh, girls packin' blades. It sounded kind of exciting. I didn't have enough sense to be scared. Turns out only two Puerto Rican girls had 'em, and that was because they were about to be jumped by the little *cholas* that ran their corner of the school. They got caught with them in paper bags in their lockers, and never took them on the road.

Kyle, the student who had the gun, was in the Feed the World Club. He had confided that he was an abused child. His mom was in prison somewhere in New York and his dad brought him and his brother out here to California apparently to use as punching bags and thugs in training. Once he showed us the scars from where his dad had smashed his head into the wall. Kyle was truly the funniest person I have ever met. He never stopped with the quips, and sometimes you'd just wish he'd get a job in standup and *live* ever after. He took good care of his little brother and always tried to get in the way of his dad's fist.

One day on the Thursday before we were to take the Feed the World Club on a camping trip, he came up to my desk, handed me a loaf of white bread in a plastic bread bag, and said, "Here, Mrs. Demerson, take care of this for me." For some reason, I guess I didn't have enough sense to question it, I took the bag and hid it in my desk drawer.

A few minutes into the period, he excused himself with a pass to the restroom. As soon as he was out of range, a very outgoing girl rushed to my desk and whispered loudly, "Miss Demerson, Kyle has a *gun!*"

"A gun??" I whispered back.

"Yeah, and he's headed for the quad!"

I got on the phone with the principal's secretary and said, "Kyle's got a gun and he's headed for the quad!"

"He's got a what?" she asked incredulously.

"A *gun!*" I whispered urgently. "And he's headed for the quad."

"I'll get Mr. Davis," she offered confidently... Sam Davis, vice principal, was All American in track. The kids all knew not to *run* from Sam Davis. So then I start to muse... hmm... Why did he tell Samantha he had the gun?

After I asked her, she told me Kyle had said, "Look what I have in my pocket." And she did, and she saw the gun. Samantha, without a doubt, had the biggest mouth in the school. Kyle must have wanted me to know.

Kyle got back to class. I met him outside and said, "Give me what you have in your pocket *right now*. Mr. Davis is on his way." He pulled it out and handed it to me, and I locked it in my car, parked a few yards away. We went back to class. Turns out he had been thrown on his butt in the common room by a bunch of huge Samoan boys the day before. This was no small feat because

Kyle was a big strong kid. He said he just wanted the word to go out that he had *brought* a gun to school.

Hence, Samantha.

"Here, Mrs. Demerson, take care of this for me."

I think those words meant, "I am about to get myself into trouble." The bread was a metaphor for his need. I'm so glad I was listening for his inner thoughts. And so glad Samantha had passed along her concerns.

We Are the World

Hip-hop was in full swing and rap was taking hold. We were inspired by the music of "Feed the World," by the British Band-Aid concert, and by Quincy Jones' production of "We Are the World," a beautiful song with the highest profile pop stars singing in unison. As a group, we decided to create a music video that we could use to promote awareness and recruit new members. The core group was very tightly knit because we had only one purpose: to help those less fortunate, thus making the music video so fulfilling.

I asked the students to "dream" their vision of what the video should be like. One young woman who remains dear to me came up with the idea to show them—the students—as themselves first, and then show them changing into hapless homeless people, or poor mothers from Ethiopia, or victims of the Vietnam War. We wanted to use music from a popular rap group called "Full Force," who were made famous in the House Party movies of the eighties. Their song "Dream Believer" inspired the scenes. We heard that in order to avoid copyright infringement, using over eight bars of an artist's music required written permission. So I wrote Full Force and asked them. Their *mother* called me at school during class.

"My sons said they would be proud to have their music used in the video to help stop world hunger."

I could barely contain my excitement and yelled out to the class: "I'm talking to Full Force *Mom!*" She sent us their written permission, and we were off! We made the video with twelve dollars in our budget, which we used for some fake flowers for the set and a couple of other props. My husband's cousin had a public television show, and our goal was to get the video on television there, and on a local Saturday morning teen show hosted by the daughter of famous poet Imamu Amiri Baraka.

My husband's cousin, Queen Ann Cannon, who is a local activist for every African American group you could name and seemed to know everyone, suggested that if we paid her cameraman a hundred dollars, he would film with a real television camera. That was exciting, so we raised the money from candy sales (ironic since we were campaigning against malnutrition). We learned that to make a music video, one has to have a split-page script, timed, with what is going to happen visually on the left and what will happen with sound concurrently on the right side of the page. So writing the script was shared by the most darling script-writer ever. Her name was Valerie, and I shall never forget her courage and her creativity, but most of all I shall not forget her sense of joy in the midst of sadness. She was simply irrepressible!

Valerie was a diminutive Mexican-American girl who could steal your heart—an odd expression since her heart was both spiritually and physically at the heart of my memories of her. Valerie lived with an abusive mother. Valerie had open-heart surgery which had left a large scar on her chest. It was frightening to me to know that such a sweet, thoughtful, and intelligent girl could have been through so much at such an early age. We spent 108 hours (!) on the video script, so long that the club began to feel like a family. With my daughters in tow, we had gone from set to set and staged our ideas. We showed the finished video to all the freshman social studies classes, hoping to increase membership and raise awareness. The video was a great success and helped us to recruit for many subsequent years.

I was asked to present our club's achievements at the California State Social Studies Convention. Since I had never learned to speak publicly without breaking out in cold sweat pouring down my sides and crying, I asked my husband what I should do. He told me emphatically, "If what you have to say is important enough, you just have to do it!" So I took his advice to heart and began to try to desensitize myself to possible criticism. Charles had said to start small with a local group of trusted friends, so I volunteered at every faculty meeting and staff development to be the presenter for my group. It started to go better and better, but I was still terrified to give a workshop for adults. Funny how it was so easy to talk in front of teenagers, and so daunting to do so in front of peers!

I expressed my fears to one of my freshman classes. Aaron, a boy who to this day ranks as one of those most brilliant students I have ever met, explained a method that also helped. He said, "Mrs. Demerson, ya just take a poster and ya put the topics you're gonna cover in a big clock face. Then ya take a ruler and ya start pointin' ta twelve o'clock and work your way around the clock face. The ruler is so ya have somethin' ta do with your hands. Then when ya get back ta twelve o'clock, you're done!" By god, it worked.

I used my husband's and Aaron's advice and took my own advice as well, as I hauled two girls along with me to the Social Studies Convention, to stand on either side of me as I presented, all of us in our Feed the World sweatshirts. They were there to catch me if I fell down. I didn't fall down. And the relief has carried me forward so that I never hesitated from that day on to speak up and represent.

As we entered the ladies' bathroom at the luxury Fairmont Hotel where the convention was held, we chorused, "Oh My God.

This bathroom is better than my living room!" We all said it at the exact same time. We burst into laughter and I realized that living a modest lifestyle in their neighborhood helped me to be a teacher who could truly relate. And such loving bonds were formed. Those two girls were the same pair who'd "packed blades" in the locker room. Yet here we were at the Fairmont, acting as though we belonged.

The club was multiracial, and happily, everyone enjoyed each other's company. As a group, we staged a Pretend Prom when prom time rolled around that year, because none of the club members had enough money to buy the prom bid, rent the tux, or get a limo or nice car. My husband and I dressed up fancy, too, and we all went to the Santa Cruz Beach Boardwalk, which was deserted at that off-season time. Charles and I renewed our vows, and the kids danced and cavorted in fancy clothes. It was delightful. Later one of the moms commented, when looking at the pictures, that all the couples were mixed, ethnically. Nobody had really planned that! There was a Vietnamese boy with a Black girl, a Vietnamese girl with a Black boy, a Salvadoran girl with a Black boy, a Mexican girl with a Filipino boy, and white me with my Black husband. It became a moment of pride with us that we had set an example of successful interracial love.

One night my Uncle Homer was visiting us at our home in East San José. He had lived in Afghanistan and Pakistan for many years as part of the USAID (United States Aid to Agriculture), helping farmers to increase their crop yield. Our house was only three blocks from Overfelt High School. (Kind of in the ghetto-y part of town where crackheads might knock at your door and ask for twenty bucks to fix "a tire.") He had spoken with my Feed the World kids earlier that day at my school, explaining to them about the famine where he had recently been advising farmers in Africa. His information was inspiring—that we could, in fact, reclaim the deserts that devastated Africa; that it would be physically possible. The only obstacle: the need to remove all the people off the given region. At that time, the people of Western

Somalia were taking in refugees by the thousands in an effort to provide relief to others in famine. Perhaps the world would come to its senses and organize a greening of the deserts.

Uncle Homer had many experiences abroad, but few with neighborhoods like East San José. His perspective was important to me and I hope for the club as well, and seeing things through his eyes was fascinating. I still wonder what he thought about what happened next.

As we enjoyed our evening back at home with just family, though my husband was at work at his night job, a knock came at the door. I opened it to find little Valerie on the doorstep wheezing and clutching her chest.

"My *heart*, Mrs. Demerson, my *heart!*" she gasped, telling me that her mom had been chasing her to beat her, and she had jumped out the window and run the four blocks to my house.

I ushered her in to lie on the couch, yelling "Call 9-1-1! Call 9-1-1!" While on the phone with dispatch, I kept stuttering the address repeatedly because I was so scared, not realizing they would automatically have that. I kept thinking that her surgery had only been four months ago and maybe she was having a heart attack. It was a very stressful time until fire trucks zoomed up and paramedics arrived. They checked her out, and she was O.K. Then about *five* police cars showed up. I guess that was SOP. But why? The situation had been handled.

In strode the cops, and they hung around interrogating Valerie as though she were a suspect instead of a hapless teenager. We had called her boyfriend, who happened to be eighteen, (she was sixteen or seventeen), and he had arrived for moral support. He was talking quietly to her. The police claimed they had spoken with the mom, who wanted to press charges on Valerie's boyfriend! They also marched themselves around my house as though it were theirs. One cop went into our garage conversion where my husband had a universal gym and some other workout equipment. That, along with our sizeable library of books, completely filled the room.

He yelled out to the female cop, "Hey, come in here and check out these weights!"

I commented, "That's my *husband's* workout room."

This did not stop them from sitting on his leg press and helping themselves to a trial of the weight room. Meanwhile, another cop began interrogating the boyfriend and insinuating that he was some type of criminal. It was all very ugly. Poor Valerie had explained why she had run, despite her racing heart. It was a lesson to me that reinforced my skeptical attitude towards police. I think it was an eye-opener for my Uncle Homer as well to see how American cops acted towards Mexicans in a neighborhood like ours. It was a lesson to me that teachers' jobs don't stop at the English lesson. We are TC and TC. Take Care and Take Charge. If we are seen as good teachers, kids turn to us as friends in times of crisis. Are we ready for that?

Through it all, Valerie kept her spirit.

The stories of the individuals in Feed the World Club go on and on. While it was rewarding, it was also draining. By the time we finished the music video, and that year wore on, several of us had suffered life-changing sadness. We asked the school to provide us with a group counselor, so we could take some time to talk about our life events and commiserate with one another. Sitting in a circle, they each shared a sadness that was keeping them up at night. I am glad that I cannot remember them all. Does that sound heartless? It was just too much. We were all crying, and I think the counselor was amazed at how well we were comforting each other, kind of without her help.

Then Valerie looked at me and said, in that inimical sweet voice of hers that used to brag about her many "*Awards!*" "…and Mrs. Demerson, my cat died."

I burst into sobbing gasping tears, at which point she said, "*Just kidding*! Oh my God, Mrs. Demerson, I was just kidding!"

We all combusted into laughter. It was just what we needed. I hugged Valerie tightly. That cathartic experience helped us all keep from the precipice of depression and despair and helped us to honor our sadness as we shared our humanity. The club continued for several years. I shall never forget the experience of the Feed the World Club, and I carry them all in my "Special Moments" photo album where all the pictures are out of focus due to my lack of skill and my "ghetto" camera, and in my Special Moments part of my heart. I've kept the music video, and the sweatshirt as well.

Chapter 6. Depression

Some say they hate to see a grown man cry. I hate to see a grown man cry convulsively from depression. Crying out of empathy is wonderful to see. Once when passing around an old photograph of a slave with extreme scars from beatings, one young Filipino man could not speak but simply beat his right fist across his chest to his heart and looked into my eyes with huge tears welling up. This is the kind of crying one wants to see. If we could all see through this young man's eyes, through our tears, the world would be a better place. But the kind of crying I never want to see is the tears like these young people shed.

Thien

One year at Yerba Buena, I had to share my classroom due to campus overcrowding. So during my "prep" period, when teachers are supposed to be able to prepare for other classes, another teacher was in my room teaching a sophomore honors English class. I enjoyed observing what was occurring around me as I tried to grade papers or write something for a lesson, because my colleague's style was laid-back and personable, and we got along wonderfully. I respected her knowledge, and she mine. In the back sat a young Vietnamese boy who was impossible not to notice because he had unusual blue eyes— there were probably five other students at Yerba Buena with blue eyes, all of whom were white. This boy responded well to the teacher, seemed happy, well-adjusted, and contributed and interacted normally. The following year, the boy was assigned to my junior (not honors) English class. First, I asked why he hadn't taken Honors English III. He gave the usual reason: he had heard the teacher was way too hard with homework. Sometimes I wonder if the student who uses this as an excuse is lazy. But in this kid's case, being lazy was definitely not the problem. Although responsive as usual at the beginning of the term, his class participation and grade began to fall. I was wondering what was going on, but it happens, and sometimes there is just nothing to be done. I planned to intervene with suggestions at some point.

Several days in a row, this boy was in my room at lunch with his head in his arms on the desk, I presumed sleeping. One day I saw his back heaving and realized he was crying. I immediately went to sit at the desk next to his and asked what was wrong. As the story unfolded, I heard something I would never forget, a testament to the unsung teenager—the teenager whose love and sacrifice holds power beyond imagining. This boy, whom I will call Thien, explained through his tears and sobbing, that he was now failing most of his classes after having had a 4.0 grade point average through sophomore year. "What's going on with you?" I calmly asked. Here is the story he told:

"My dad is gone to Vietnam. He hates us. He beats my mom when he is home, so we are glad he is gone. But my sister is on drugs, and she is off living in her car. She left behind her little baby boy. He sleeps with me. He's like fifteen months old now, and he has always slept with me. My mom works all the time and doesn't have time to take care of him. So I have to. I love him, and I won't give him up. My sister won't come home to take him. Now I have to move into my car because things are going wrong at home. He's my boy now, and I won't give him up. I don't know what I am going to do. When I was a kid, I used to watch sitcoms on TV and think, *If only we were a white family. Then we could be happy like those families on TV.*"

This is depression.

I called the family services clinic and apprised them of the situation. Thien continued sporadic attendance and would usually be in the room stoically and silently crying at lunch, during which time I would just listen and try to understand. I would check in with family services to see if anything were being done, and they always told me they were aware of the situation and doing what they could. One day I realized Thien was no longer coming at all. I called family services, academic counseling, other teachers, and no one knew where he was or what had happened. I contacted Asian Americans for Community Involvement, the agency that works with the school, but they had no trace.

I will never forget the love that poured out of that boy's heart for his little nephew. I will never forget that fifteen-year-olds can be more than adult. And I will never stop wondering what happened to Thien.

José

The first day of school, I posed my usual beginning-of-the-year homework question: If the Earth is an orange on my desk, how far away is the sun, and how big is it? Followed by: If the Earth is an orange on my desk, how far away is the moon, and how big is it? The next day we discussed the answers they brought in, and it gave me a good idea of who did homework and who didn't; who knew how to use Google and who didn't; who would respond with Yahoo Answers that were only tangentially related to the question; who could do advanced math. This is good insight for a teacher. But my real aim was to get the students to begin to wonder at the vastness of space and our place in it. José brought the most interesting response, as he was the first to state that he had gone outside, looked at the night sky, and contemplated the question.

José's tears could fill channels. He cried angry tears in my room at breaks, the kind I could only hope would help to purge the resentment. As his dad was beating his mom, José ran into the street, fell on his knees, and screamed to God to help his family. He was a thoughtful boy, and it seemed that his depression would overwhelm all the star-gazing he was once capable of. He, too, left our school, never to be heard from again. His family had owned a little *joyeria*, or jewelry store, in our East Side neighborhood. Every time I passed a *joyeria*, I would think of that boy alone and screaming in the streets, cursing his dad and praying for help.

Ms. Z

I had Ms. Z in a class at Overfelt High School called the "Opportunity Program." Our associate principal in charge of discipline used to call it the "Lack of Opportunity Program." He believed, and I understand why, that the students who were not taking advantage of regular classes to pass and get a diploma should not be given Extra Opportunity. But at least he gave them one more chance. The program was designed with the physical education teacher/football coach as one teacher, and me as the other, based in a two-classroom portable building on campus. We taught the students all of their subjects, with Mr. Figueroa teaching math and P.E., and my teaching English and study skills. We also had the help of Mr. Phinney, who taught history. The kids used to call the coach "Fig." So kids would call them Fig and Phinney.

(Once my sister asked me, "Just who are these Fin and Figgy people you keep talking about?" *"Ha!* No, Dear, it's Fig and Phinney.")

Students were placed in the program if they had gone through the year before with horrible attendance and failing grades, often with behavior problems as well. We hoped to give them a more comfortable learning environment by helping them to bond with other students with similar problems, and by giving them fewer teachers to have to deal with. It turns out the one thing they all had in common was that they had failed P.E. Often this was because of lack of attendance, but it was also because of body image. Some were obese and refused to dress out. Some were too shy to dress out. Having P.E. with only each other, just playing a game of their choice in their regular clothes, seemed to bring physical education within their reach of capability, and soon all were passing the class.

Students who had attended *no days* the year before were suddenly reaching perfect attendance levels. They were passing perfunctory exams in their subjects and getting high school credits. Other teachers complained that the standards weren't high enough in the program, but what did they know? Students were *not* joining the program to get out of work. If a student did not have serious problems or exhibit the behaviors of what I called "The Walking Wounded," they would want to get out of the program before two weeks were up. Because being in a room all day with these students was way too draining for a student capable of attending regular classes! The bottom line was, students who before had problems that seemed insurmountable were experiencing new successes in many areas, and the program was working. So of course the district said, "Thank you very much, but we're discontinuing your Opportunity Program."

Ms. Z was a young lady who was in the program because she had a serious drinking problem that kept her home for too many days the year before. This was a girl with depression – or I should say Depression with a capital *D*.

Her brother told me about her depression, a story that would leave many of us feeling desperate as well.

Ms. Z was a teenage mother with no baby. The year before, she had asked her parents if she could go and live with an aunt who lived some distance away, so that they never really saw each other during that school year. She had been pregnant. While she lived with the aunt, she delivered a healthy baby girl, whom the aunt adopted as her own. Ms. Z was now seventeen, living back with her parents, who never knew about the baby. Now she drank heavily to drown the sorrow of her loss. The little girl who was being raised as her cousin was really hers. I often wonder if she would ever recover. We did what we could in the Opportunity Program, but where were her Opportunities?

How do kids like these study? How do they go on? Sometimes they don't. Teen suicide has affected almost every school district in the country. How do we know when a young person will make it out of the morass of true depression? It's hard enough to face the abyss, the existential crisis when most people realize they are in this life alone. But to face situations like Thien's, José's, and Ms. Z's... Who could "deal"?

One of my current Facebook friends who was a sweet student in my first period class constantly threatens suicide. He began to threaten when I was teaching my last semester before retirement. I was quite upset because a colleague of mine was also nearing the brink, and I felt overwhelmed with responsibility to report and to make sure they were getting professional help. It was an incredibly difficult and emotional end to my career. Not only did I worry about the potential suicides, but other students were behaving oddly. These things would test me and my resolve to give until I couldn't afford to give any more. Depression can be contagious. As an educator, it is always a challenge to stay accessible, yet just detached enough, so that we can persevere and maintain mental health. Or at least a semblance of it.

As I was beginning a job at a school for emotionally disturbed children—the Spring Branch Academy in Texas—my brother said, "Hannah Lynn, the problem with teaching a mentally disturbed teenager is you have to *stop being* a mentally disturbed teenager!"

And he was in a position to know, as he had achieved his PhD with Phi Beta Kappa awards and was a licensed family psychologist!

As mandated reporters, teachers have to fill out Child Protective

Services reports on kids we even suspect are being abused or hurting themselves. This definitely tests us as professionals because we know that the student's family will be investigated. In some cases, students are immediately removed to the "shelter" by uniformed police and not permitted to return home. I learned this the hard way, after a beautiful girl raised her shirt to reveal parallel-striped weals about two inches wide lining her abdomen and lower chest. Her dad had decided a garden stake beating would straighten her out. Just as I feared, uniformed police officer removed her from school and took her to the children's shelter. She was not allowed to go home. And we have all heard horror stories of what goes on in the "shelters." The "shelter" in San José was subsequently shut down after the discovery of rampant sexual relations among "sheltered" kids.

How to make a judgment call on the choice to report? One girl at the continuation school told me that her father used to slap her. It had just slipped out and she begged me not to tell. I reminded her of my status as mandated reporter, and that if she told me anything more, I would be reporting it as abuse. Did she think it reached the level of abuse? "No, No, Mrs. Demerson, and he doesn't do it anymore, and I really don't want you to report!" At this point I told her that if she thought about it later and changed her mind and/or mentioned it to anyone else, they would report, and I would corroborate that I had heard it as well. She told the same story to a different teacher (whom I trusted) later in the day. The teacher was furious with me for not reporting it, even after I explained my choice. This was her choice, yet if I had it to do over again, I would have said and done the same thing. I believed in the young person's autonomy more than I believed in regulations. At some point, one's experience must guide actions. The existential moral imperative is to take whatever consequences may ensue and do whatever work is necessary to create the best outcome one is able to achieve. I volunteered to do the paperwork to Child Protective Services. The young lady herself was not upset with me and appreciated that I had given her a chance to think about it. And a choice.

One boy begged me not to report his abusive parents, but since he had written his story on a college field trip application, I had no choice, and in his case, it was best that I did. He continued to say he didn't want anyone else involved, but chose to be my aide the following year, and continues to seek my advice on Facebook. At one point he looked out at my class and said something to the effect that if they had a problem, they could tell Mrs. Demerson because she *would* take care of it. That's when I knew my intervention had helped.

Sometimes just letting kids know you're on *their* team builds very strong bridges towards mental health. When I was a teenager myself, I went to counseling in Indianapolis. When I arrived for the first time at the center, an older man, an intake psychologist, read my application, simply walked up to me, touched me lightly on the shoulder, and said, "You just want to feel better." The flood of tears that burst out took me quite by surprise. It was such a simple acknowledgement, yet it touched something deep inside me that needed release. We can offer at least that.

The Unfinished Business—the Child Left Behind

Policies—first implemented then *unfunded* to the tune of billions of dollars by George W. Bush—stated that No Child [would be] Left Behind. This policy clearly meant No Child Left Behind Whose Parents Make More Than $200,000 a Year. I am here to tell you that some children will be left behind.

I remember a girl named Jennifer whose sad little face still haunts my memories. Despite everything I or her fellow students could do, I do not think that little heart-shaped face managed a smile for the entire year in my class. Her half-sister explained some of the family problems, and I could understand why the sadness. I did have chats with her, seeking to help, but her depression was somewhere deeper than all my love and concern could reach.

My colleagues and I attended a voluntary training called TESA – Teacher Expectation, Student Achievement, where we saw a film called *Cipher in the Snow*. It was an evocative film about a young student whom no one saw. It is the invisible, quiet child who never rocks the boat. Because of class size and teacher overload, we do not blame any individual teacher. But this child literally died in the snow next to a school bus, leaving a curious curve that looked, when seen from above, as though she had laid out the letter *C*, attempting an aborted message. As the camera zoomed out at the end of the film, most of us felt changed. We wanted to ensure that those quiet children we taught did not become ciphers in the snow.

I feared that Jennifer would remain the invisible child. She wasn't, to me. I referred her for counseling and put her exquisite handwritten work on the bulletin board just to see it for myself. Sometimes now I see her post about a happy college event on Facebook, and I breathe a little more easily. But sometimes children are left behind. How many Jennifers did I miss?

Chapter 7. Drug Use and Other Missteps

There are some funny things about drug abuse. My daughters told me that the police officers who came to their high school with the DARE to Keep Kids Off of Drugs Program showed them a suitcase full of drugs and explained their use. The girls told me that it made the drugs sound really fun to try! Later while watching the TV program *Reno 9-1-1*, we all burst out laughing at their depiction of a Deputy Dog man in a dog suit with similar outcomes. Efforts to dissuade children from drug use or to educate them about "stranger danger" were woefully inadequate in most cases and even ludicrous at times.

There are some sad stories about drug abuse, but I think my sense of humor has developed now to the point where I can laugh about some drug stories, because as far as I know, the kids involved still survive. The key to humor in a dark place is to see our absurdity in the face of desperate circumstances, and to take joy in survival! One Black friend from Harlem told me that the funniest thing in the world to him was when someone almost died, but then they didn't. At the time I thought this was horrible and wanted him to "take it back." But he explained that when they were young, their friends and family members were often victims of police brutality and were victims of police profiling as a matter of course. As teenagers, he and his friends would go up on the roof of their tenement apartment buildings and slide a large metal garbage can off the edge of the roof, to land *just* behind a beat cop as he walked his beat underneath. At the telling of this, he burst into uncontrollable laughter! I thought he would choke and die! He then morphed into a very, very serious expression and yelled: "Now *that* is funny." As I imagined the sound of that garbage can smacking into the street—that would be a shock that could turn your hair white—and I thought about the teens laughing at their power, I began to understand.

My husband shares that perspective. I never saw anyone laugh as hard as Charles did at one drug-related incident with our foster boys when we were group home parents. Without going into detail about the group home parent experience, let me say that these boys had issues – or *issues*. The ones with *issues* were the ones who were addicted to inhalants. They couldn't get their hands on their usual drugs, so they were resorting to spraying paint into lockers and sticking their heads in. When we nipped that in the bud, they found liquid correction fluid, or "Wite-Out," in a baggie held up to their mouths and noses would do the trick. When confronted, they would look at us with glazed eyes and slurred speech, saying, "Nah, man, I didn't do nothing," all the while the little white dots of correction fluid were clearly visible on their upper lips! Charles would find them sneaking into the family room at night, watching slasher movies. He cautioned them over and over. "Y'all better stop gettin' high watchin' them horror movies, 'cause I'm *tellin'* ya, that shit gets in your *head*. It has a *turrible* effect on your brain." One night as we lay sleeping, all of a sudden, we heard a loud thump, thump—and screaming.

We ran into the hallway to find two of the teenage boys holding their heads, rocking back and forth yelling, "Oh, *God*, Oh, *God!*"

We asked, "What happened? What's wrong?"

"Ah, man, Charles, we saw these big monsters zooming straight for us, so we ran into the closet!" They had found and taken more inhalants and were ambushed by a shared hallucination of the horrors they had watched, so they tried to run *right through the wall*! I thought my husband was going to literally burst his sides laughing, *screaming* and rolling on the couch, tears pouring down his face, laughing so hard he fell on the floor. *"I told y'all not to do that! Y'all been gettin' high, watchin' that horror shit again! I told y'all! I told y'all!"* To Charles, the sheer folly of that sequence of consequences was indescribably funny. I had seen enough to know that there was nothing much left to do *but* laugh. And he looked so funny rolling off that couch.

Lest I sound too insensitive to drug problems, I must say the foster care system was providing "help" in the form of a slick city fellow who drove up in a red Corvette and was introduced as the psychologist who was going to perform drug counseling for our foster boys. The boys took one look at the man and his car and they had him conned immediately. They washed his car and then began taking advantage of him, from lying outright to getting him to give them money. It obviously was no fast-track to rehabilitation.

One boy did come back to visit us years later. He was clean and sober for a year, had a wife and an eight-year-old son. and was gainfully employed. He had often stared at us when he was in our group home, saying, "Wow. I never knew anybody before who would actually have a *discussion* about what was on TV." He came to thank me, and especially Charles, for changing his life. He told Charles, "Man, I never told you this before, but my dad in prison was in Aryan Nation. You changed me. I even had a Black girlfriend for a while."

Once at a graduate seminar for teachers, I mentioned making fun of really sweet, introverted honors kids by calling them crack addicts. It always brings a laugh because I pick the least likely student to take drugs and call her that. Then everyone can picture their pre-conceived notions turned upside-down, and it's funny. I still tease one of my former students, who is now a graduate of university, about the time she mugged the ice cream truck driver. It so obviously wasn't true, but a fellow student had said that about her in an essay that she read out loud to the class. *Everyone* laughed, especially she, because of the notion that this sweet girl could ever be a thug. Once I saw the kids eating Pop-Tarts without heating them up first. I went home and asked my daughter if she thought anyone would eat Pop-Tarts cold. She immediately came back with, "Yeah, if they're on *crack*!" So ever after, if I saw a kid with a cold Pop-Tart, I would say, "Stop takin' that *crack*!" If a student forgets something five minutes after he has said it, I usually say, "You *need* to stop smokin' that *weed*."

So at the graduate seminar for teachers, an eighth-grade teacher overheard my saying something about this, and asked my friend in horror, "Does she really talk about crack with her students? I would *never* talk about drugs with my students."

Oh My God! What planet are you from? When they told us the three things never to talk about were sex, politics, and religion, did you listen to that crap advice as well? Because those are three of the only things *worth talking about*! If you don't feel up to the job, why are you a teacher? These are the things that matter, really matter to students. If you are unclear yourself about where you stand, it's OK to say that. But avoiding key topics is shirking your most sacred responsibility. To help adolescents confront and explore *life* in its myriad permutations, to aid them in making life's most difficult choices, and to remind them of life's most rewarding possibilities—that is a critical area where teachers can excel. Drugs are padding to protect from the jabs of a cruel life. They should be openly discussed and given gravitas when kids are in crisis, but levity as well, when that is what is needed.

The schools where I taught and the neighborhood where we lived were once called the PCP capital of the world. If you are unaware of the effects of this drug, imagine your child taking a tranquilizer meant for elephants. Brain damage.

One Samoan student I had said his name was Evil. He said if I didn't believe he was a good graffiti artist, take a look at the overpass on Jackson Ave. Sure enough, as I drove up Jackson one day, there was his name EVIL in graffiti letters five feet high. He said he had taken a lot of PCP, and it was hard for him to concentrate. He used to draw graffiti all over the room. I encouraged him to continue, by having him sit right next to me, facing the class, where I could shovel paper after paper under those fidgety hands, so he could keep the graffiti going and I wouldn't have to clean it up. He began to listen more in class and to participate occasionally when he could bring his eyes into focus to read for a short period of time. He was always respectful to me.

I decided to make friends of the Samoan students first, since they were the biggest and most stand-offish students at the school. With them on my side, I felt like some really good kids "had my back." Some of them would actually come to my class twice in the same day: once at their scheduled time, and once during their open period, just to hang out. I started the practice of having them "be me," by remembering the lesson and replicating it later. The second class to have the lesson was often more enthralled with a lesson from their peer than they were to hear it coming from me. It was a win-win. After all, they usually only listen to each other anyway, this way at least they were getting the content I wanted them to get, and it was more fun for all of us.

The friendships came in handy one day when a kid named Uzi (named after a family of Israeli open-bolt, blowback-operated submachine guns. Really?) challenged me and said he was going to "...go home and get my Uzi and come back for you." Why? Because I had supervised at a dance the night before: I had a front row seat to a fight that Uzi started with a kid named J.J. Uzi and J.J. were broken apart by security at the dance, but as I passed through the quad the next day, I overheard Uzi bragging. I turned around to stare. He asked me what I was doing, and I said, "I'm just listening to hear if you tell the story the way I saw it." The much larger Samoan boy to whom he was spinning his yarn was an ally of mine from one of my classes the year before. After Uzi made his threat, the other boy said, "Nah, man, don't mess with her, she's cool." I breathed. I went on to class and called the associate principal to relate the threat. He told me, "That's OK, Mrs. Demerson, he already had four toes out the door. This is the fifth. Just write it up." Uzi was expelled. I felt a strange sense of calm about the whole thing. Still not sure if I should have been more scared.

The intersection of King and Story, a low-rider area, was a few blocks from our house. It was well-known to be a gang neighborhood with lots of drugs. Crack cocaine entered the scene, and some of the next generation of students would be affected by having had crack-addicted parents. I remember one of my students, a beautiful twin, was a crack addict, and she had a child at fifteen. I could have been teaching her grandchildren by the time I retired. One crack-addicted couple had two sons, both of whom were named the same name. I guess they forgot they had already used that name. As it turned out, both of the children became my students and my neighbors across the street when a loving relative took them in after both of their parents were hauled off to prison on drug charges. Tragically, that loving woman got cancer, and those boys agonized through watching the only one who truly cared for them suffer, waste away, and die while they were still trying to finish high school. I recommended them to a temporary homeschool teacher the district could provide, since obviously they could not concentrate in class.

I have met many, many grandparents who are raising the children of their drug-addicted children. My hat is off to them, as I cannot imagine how difficult it must be to know that the person you raised cannot function, and now you must start all over again, in an aging body that has already performed its parenting role. And often those grandchildren are born with addiction and suffer from ADHD or other nervous disorders as a result. My husband and I know firsthand how inadequate at best, and destructive at worst, the foster system can be. So when relatives can take these drug-involved children, it is usually a preferred outcome. I have had few phone-call relationships with parents, but grandparents who are raising these kids are the ones I most enjoy talking to and helping whenever I can.

Rohypnol, the so-called Date Rape Drug, also made its rounds as a drug of choice for some teens. I remember a girl sauntering into class, walking unsteadily and swaying her hips salaciously from the back to the front of the room, with a ridiculous sideways smile on her face, slurring her words, being laughed at uproariously by the class. They yelled out "Pinga! Pinga!" which was slang Mexican Spanish for her condition (not a nice term). She seemed to be having the time of her life. It was easy to see how she could have been taken advantage of. But for the moment, I'm sure she was feeling no pain. Everyone seemed to think it was a great joke. But I still had to report it.

And alcohol problems? Very prevalent among kids in our community. Parents even hosted keggers (beer-keg parties) for their teen kids sometimes. Once while teaching in the Opportunity Program, I was given a lesson in at-school alcohol abuse. The coach who taught next door used to let the students who had perfect attendance all week watch a movie of their choice on Friday morning. I did not agree with the choice idea, since watching Tom Cruise tend bar and womanize was not my idea of education. But it certainly was a motivation for the kids to attend Monday through Thursday. They also were allowed popcorn and sodas. One Monday I was in the middle of a lesson, showing a video that was not a movie, when two male teachers abruptly opened *my* classroom door and turned off *my* video presentation to commence yelling at the students. It seems one of the girls in the class had gone to the basketball game the Friday night before and had fallen down drunk in front of the bleachers. As staff attended to her, she yelled out that yes, she was drunk, and she had been drinking since that morning *in Mrs. Demerson's class!*

My eyes must have popped into saucers as I sputtered, "Whaaaa?" Apparently since I had watched the class briefly that Friday morning to spell the other teacher, she got the notion that it had been my class in which they had been drinking. An honest mistake, a drunken utterance, but a huge embarrassment to me. It came out that the students had been regularly spiking their two-liter bottles of soda with alcohol every movie morning. Those little dickens, as my mom would say. There is really no way to come back from that. Some people will always think I allowed drinking in class. The movies were eventually reinstated without the snacks and drinks, but I never won the argument about the type of movie to be shown. And those two male teachers were not justified in disrespecting me like that. I did tell them, but it wasn't the first time, and it wouldn't be the last. I'm saving the rest of the staff disrespect stories for Part II of this narrative. I would even be embarrassed to have a student see me in a public restaurant with a bottle of wine in front of me. That was not the image I wanted young people to have of me, at all.

Many students made the mistake of thinking that since I wore my hippie or bohemian style as a badge of honor, that I probably took drugs. "Peace, love, and happiness" does not mean drug abuse, people.

I learned from a communication class at the university that one can re-direct interest from the personal to the general quite easily. It is important for teachers to learn to do this, to take the focus away from your personal life and put it where it belongs, on guiding students in a useful direction.

So when they ask if I was a hippie, I say, "What do you mean *was*? Peace, love, and happiness, baby, and I will stand by that 'til I die." I straighten up my spine and flash the peace sign, looking in their eyes with intensity.

Then they will inevitably ask if I smoke weed and do drugs.

I stop class at that moment for the teaching opportunity. I take a deep breath and say, "You know, when students ask me that, I always tell them that it is not important what I did, what is important is the paradigm, or way of looking at things, that I used, to make my decisions about drugs. I always ask myself, 'Am I going to be in complete control of my thoughts? Because I don't like the feeling of being out of control. Do I want to risk having to deal with police? Am I going to be able to act quickly if someone needs my help? Am I going to be able to have healthy children?' All of these things are what helped me to make decisions about drugs, and *these* are the things you should be wondering about, too. So choose your path while looking through those glasses at the world and its consequences."

Once I've given that little talk, the students rarely ask me again.

When I went to teach at Overfelt High School for my first credentialed job, the administration placed me in an assignment mid-year. The teacher who had preceded me had transferred to another campus. I was waiting for my CBEST scores, the scores the state requires for a teacher to teach solo in a classroom. So I had the job but couldn't teach for the first six weeks of the semester. The classes had been assigned to a substitute teacher who had put his feet up and read a newspaper for those six weeks, while apparently students in the sixth period class had been rolling joints in the back row! So this is what goes on when you don't pay attention.

As I took the reins, it helped that I already had a glimpse of what young people were capable of. One colleague had described that sixth period as a zoo. I felt offended on their behalf, because whenever a white man calls minorities animals with that smirk on his face, my blood curdles. But I also relied on a wonderful colleague, Ms. Sharlene Mello, whose help was the antidote to his caustic attitude. She simply said, "I know that's a tough group you've got there, so if you ever feel you just can't take it, I will substitute for you and you can go home early." I remembered her kindness and paid it forward, encouraging all the English teachers to do the same for one another. This kind of support can mean the difference between survival and defeat in your first years. Ms. M.D., another magical antidote to negativity, encouraged me to help young teachers by volunteering to take a kid into our class when a teacher was struggling to keep the rest of them in line because of that one kid. Once the kid is transported to another class where he or she is in unknown waters, the behavior disappears. At least for that one day the teacher can breathe. And let us never underestimate the value of a "teacher bestie": a friend to grab a lunch with and to share stories!

I was determined to do what I could to calm the waters in that sixth-period class at Overfelt. I remember their erratic behavior like it was yesterday. It was the stuff of back-to-school nightmares. They were used to getting high before, after, and apparently sometimes during class. They were a class called Language Arts II. This was supposed to mean that their skills were two levels below a class whose skills were approximately on grade level. It actually meant they were incapable of writing a complete paragraph in English. Some were Special Education, some were second language learners, and some just didn't "do school." What a mix. The behaviors were often so preposterously over the top, a person would have to see it to believe it. In conference with another teacher, I found out that a boy called Gerome was one of three brothers who shared a common gene for class clown. The parents were beer-aholics. Their sons created problems for all their teachers.

Another boy, Ricardo, when assigned an essay on life goals, turned in a paper with this sentence: "My goal is to be massive." He was on the school's diving team briefly until his grades disqualified him. One day he stood on top of his desk and dove headfirst onto the floor. He said he was just demonstrating for the girls what he did at the diving competitions. Wow, really? For many years, that one incident featured in my back-to-school nightmare—the one we all have in August before we resume the joys of being the classroom's "Chief Cook and Bottle-Washer." Only one year in my memory did I not have that dream, and it turned out my husband had the dream for me (bless his heart)!

One girl was so academically behind that I remember her illiteracy as the most glaring warning against passing students through the grades as social advancement. How was she a sophomore? I met her at my local Wells Fargo bank one day, and guess what? She was in a teller trainee program! Do *not* ask me how.

I don't know how many of these students were on drugs at the time, but if you saw how they behaved, you would wonder what we were giving them.

I had to put that class and others like it in an amphitheater-seating arrangement. I had two concentric half circles curved away from me at the center. The girls sat in the back, one behind each boy, because if the boys were allowed to sit behind the girls, they would pester them with touching and poking at them. The girls were always squealing at one thing or another. I did not allow that class to bring anything to their desks. They had to put their hands on their desks in front of them and only work with the paper and pencil or book that I gave them. The semblance of order that had been created from chaos gave me a deep feeling of accomplishment, which helped to carry me through the challenges ahead. How did I get them to do it? By standing at the head of the class and yelling, "I know you've been getting away with a lot, but you can't show me *anything* I haven't seen before. I had the worst foster kids in Santa Clara County. I've lived with fire-setters and an eleven-year-old kid who smashed another kid's face off in the pavement! *Some*one will be left standing at the end of the year. *And it will be I!*"

Confidence is the drug that cures. Love is the drug that heals. Patience is my drug of choice.

Important Note: I did not do this alone. One needs to have an outlet and support from a discipline team. I did have to send students to the office and send a referral form explaining the class time suspension when student behavior was particularly egregious and disruptive. Our teachers' association, the East Side Teachers Association, was adamant and negotiated to cement in writing that a teacher can *suspend a student from class for the day of the insubordinate behavior, and the next day, the student cannot return to class, either.* This allowed for a cooling-off period for teacher and student, so that the class can continue unmolested. If you ever stop to wonder why you need to support unions, think about the wisdom in that one provision. And support your local school when they need to hire discipline advisors from among credentialed teaching staff.

Although sometimes advisors (and like some teachers, I might add), can be useless, lazy, ineffectual, or occasionally even predatory, most of the student advisors with whom I worked were very helpful and contributed immeasurably to the teaching environment. Support staff members like school liaisons were also invaluable assets. If you go into teaching, make friends with them. They work hard for less pay and little appreciation and usually only get to work with kids when they are at their worst.

A Few Words about Night School, Summer School, and Why Public School-Teaching Is So Difficult and Could Be So Much Easier if We Could…

In our district, night school and summer school classes were provided for students who were "down credits," not having passed their regular six classes per day at five credits per class. This was a large section of our student body. To be on a sports team, for example, one had to have a 2.0 GPA, meaning a C average.

It became clear that we had trouble excelling in sports when, as my husband put it while observing an Overfelt football game, "Looks like some of your best athletes are in the stands."

I explained that I had heard 70 percent of our football players did not "make grades." This meant in order to graduate, they would be in class sometimes four nights a week by the time they were "seniors"! Each three-hour night class made up for a week of one daytime class in terms of credits. But then, what is to keep a student from intentionally failing a day class just so they don't have to get up early for a first period class, or so they can avoid a teacher who is a hard grader or homework-assigner, and opt for a night school teacher, who might be (and usually would be) less demanding? We had to hire credentialed teachers, but sometimes night school teachers were hired catch-as-catch-can, and didn't really require much work before passing a student. Public school teachers take everyone, even those who sit and say, "I don't need to pass this class." What leverage is left? They can do whatever they want, and really, who could blame them for not trying? They have a backup replacement class!

I often taught night school classes to supplement our family income. And for one after-school class per week, the money was adequate. And here's the thing. In night school, students are there as a privilege, not as a right. Therefore, the teacher can *drop* a student for bad behavior. *What a difference this can make to the classroom environment!* We don't have to suspend them and take them back, suspend them and take them back, suspend them and take them back. Two infractions and you're gone. I would apprise students of this the first night, and behavior was *markedly* better in night school. Can a teacher make a mistake? Can a student get a reprieve? Well, yes to both, and no to both. Two examples that illustrate my point:

The Case of the Furious Mrs. Demerson

I often quote Tom Cruise from *Mission Impossible* when he said one of my favorite lines—with a scowl and a menacing tone: "'Mad? You've never *seen* [pause] *me* mad.' I will get *mad* if I hear or see you abuse one another. I will get *mad* if you act sexist, racist, or with complete disregard for each other's feelings. You will not be embarrassing each other or yourselves. I'm not havin' it."

So... one time in night school, we had just completed a unit on racial profiling and civil rights as a literature theme. Very rarely would I see a white student at Yerba Buena in the 90's, but there were a few. I happened to have had two white boys in this particular class, which was even more rare. Two at once? Wow. They seemed to have been quite nice fellows, so as we sat working in the computer lab, and I heard one say to the other, "... so then we went to that nigger next door and..." *Whoa!* I lost my mind. I lost my mind completely. I thought I was going to blow a gasket. I started screaming I don't remember what-all. I was literally spitting; I was so mad.

I told them *"Get out! Get out! You are expelled from night school! I never want to see you again!"* I went next door to my classroom and went to my desk and grabbed an eraser and threw it at the back wall. I was screaming, *"I quit! I quit teaching! I can't take it anymore! And after we just went through that whole unit on understanding!"* A few minutes after as the students sat in stunned silence and I sat fuming at my desk, I got a call from the night school principal.

He said, "Mrs. Demerson, I have two boys in here who say you kicked them out? Is that true?"

"Yes! And I am *not* taking them *back!"*

"Well, Mrs. Demerson, they are confused and say they have no idea why they were kicked out."

I replied, "Oh yes, they do. They used the word *nigger* right out loud!"

I don't remember the rest of the conversation, but I was completely determined to *stand my ground*.

Soon after, one of the young men came into class crying. "Mrs. Demerson, Mrs. Demerson, what did we do? Why are you so mad? I just don't understand?"

He looked so pathetic I began to doubt myself. "Wait a minute. Do you mean to tell me I didn't just hear you say, '...we went to that nigger next door...'?"

"*What?* Mrs. Demerson, I would *never* say that! I said '*neighbor*'"!

Oh no. Oh no. I replayed it in my head. It sounded exactly the same. Oh no. Oh no.

So here am I: "I'm sorry. Go get your buddy. You are back in night school. I will call Mr. U. and straighten it out. Sorry for the misunderstanding." We laughed and laughed. Night school re-booted. I didn't resign. Two white boys were reprieved. The rest of the class felt better. They had *seen me mad*, and it was unequivocal.

In another incident, the ending was not so happy. I had just gone through (what I thought had been) a very inspirational talk about how difficult it was for my husband to work his way through having been exposed to a very violent milieu as a youth. He was among the first Black students to be bused to an all-white school during desegregation in the 60's. He was in middle school at the time. He had to fight some white kid or other every single day just to get to class. Teachers actually told him when he would raise his hand, "We don't answer nigger questions." When he was on his way to high school, he had to fight another kid every day just to stay *out* of gangs. The football team was his gang. He was so determined to get out of the violent streets after having been to so many funerals of young people his age; and seeing so many going off to prison; and seeing one shoot himself in the head and die; and seeing guys die in his arms; and seeing a white security guard shoot an unarmed Black man in the back with blatant disregard for human life; and seeing Black students' being shot at his college campus. And yet he found a way out. He joined the Marine Corps and was sent to Viet Nam during the 1976 Fall of Saigon. Later, got his college education and made a professional life for himself and a good living for his family.

After all this, a kid in the back of the room sneeringly says, "Hey, can your husband get us 49er tickets?"

Again, I lost my mind. I was so angry; nothing could have appeased me. I kicked that kid out of night school. His parents came back the next day, and I saw a nasty picture emerging. His dad and mom begged for me to let him back in. I told them that thankfully, I did not have to give him another chance, since night school was a privilege which he had blatantly abused with his disrespectful attitude. I explained in full the incident and at least two other examples of his disrespect. At this, his mom began to cry and sob, and say, "I know how he disrespects. They both do. He and his father just call me all kinds of names and sit on the couch and do nothing!" She was a tiny Mexican-American woman who was dwarfed by her son and husband, and my heart went out to her. But the abuse by this big old boy had to stop somewhere. And it was going to stop with me.

I hoped she could take heart and see that if I let him back in, it would be further enabling his level of abuse. After all, as I tell the students while quoting the brilliant line from the movie *9 to 5* about working women, "I'm not *asking* for much. All I'm asking for is a *little* dignity and a *little respect*!" It was not a happy ending to a parent meeting. I could see she had her work cut out for her. I won't forget her or the dozens like her I would see cowering as their husbands or sons took advantage. Family is important, but empowerment for the weakest among the family is critical. If all the moms and dads showed respect for each other and their children, we would see changes in schools. But we can't go home with them to help. We can only stand firm in our own classrooms and expect, demand, and most importantly *deserve* respect ourselves.

Time for a Funny Night School Adventure

Once I got to teach a night school class for older people to show them how to use computers. Living in world-famous Silicon Valley, we knew many people in the tech world, and my husband was working at 3-Com Corporation as an IT Scheduling

Engineer. I did know the basics of using a computer, so I thought it might be fun to share the love. I actually had one of my all-time best teaching experiences doing this. The class was open to the community for over-55-year-old students. We started the class by my having them take the components apart and set them back up. This only required pulling out cords to the printers, keyboards, mice, and wall power cords, and replacing them one by one. In this fashion, I hoped to show them that they were not going to break their computer by sticking the wrong thing in the wrong hole. They learned that looking closely at the cord's end and the hole they thought it might go in would show them that they wouldn't be *able* to put it in the wrong hole. This did lead to a bit of a giggle, but more importantly, reduced their hesitation to master the machine.

It was an unbelievably fun class to teach! Upon hearing that I was chosen to teach it, my daughter who is a tech maven, commented: "Wow, did they pick you because you are just one step ahead of the students?" And that was just the ticket! I regularly referred to the fact that I had just learned this myself. It helped because I could assume the ignorance I recently had, and remember the exact steps, step by step, that it took me to learn the new skill. So when one of the older ladies told me that her son was the guy who invented the Palm Pilot, I got so mad at him because she said he couldn't teach her how to use her computer. According to her, he would go to her keyboard and quickly type a bunch of keys and *voila*! As if by magic, everything worked. But of course, he wouldn't slow down and do it step by step for her—he was too busy. (Or too impatient.) I was so happy to help her, and she was so happy to learn. Truly a win-win situation in that class. We laughed, we learned together, and always had snacks. The perfect night school class. And when some of the octogenarians would come back the next week having forgotten absolutely everything, I would not lose patience with them because they were so respectful to me! If all the students in my day classes would learn that one simple fact...

Why Summer School is so Great – Lessons from my Nine-Year-Old

In addition to having the ability to kick out any kid who isn't respectful, summer school brought with it the ideal teaching situation. I learned in Montessori teacher training that children should have choices in what they are learning, and that they should be able to take their time completing a project. In fifty-minute class periods, one never has time to see a project through to completion in one satisfying setting. In summer school, the periods are much longer, sometimes five hours in the same room. While this may seem daunting, it is pedagogically sound. As part of my early fascination with teaching, I read *Summerhill*, a book that explored schooling students in England who had not been to school for several years. They took these students into an enriched environment at the age of sixteen. They taught them everything they needed to know to pass all of their high school courses in six months. Here's how they did it. They used project-centered instruction in *one subject at time.* The students did not move to the next subject until they were immersed in and mastered the first one. If my older daughter would have had this opportunity when she struggled with fragmented learning, she would have been less likely to describe going from class to class as the feeling of her skin being scratched raw and salt being poured into the flesh once every hour! Many kids are miserable dealing with too many changes of scene and too many individuals every day, whose harsh or even subtle criticism can destroy a young person's sense of well-being.

There is a trick to successful summer school. I thought, *I cannot stand here and lecture for five hours. What should I do? These kids will drive each other, and me! crazy.*

My daughter Rainy, then nine years old and going into fifth grade, walked in to my classroom and said, "Mommy, you should do stations."

I queried, "What do you mean? What are stations?" She explained that you put the kids in groups and have one activity at each station. Give them time to complete the activity, then move the groups to the next station. So I went home and figured out an activity for each station that would take approximately the same amount of time as each of the other activities. So there was a station activity for reading and answering comprehension questions; one for vocabulary; one for grammar and usage; one for essay-writing; one for pleasure reading; and one for art, music, and poetry about art. This gave me six stations and with five kids at each station. They would sit and do their project, then I would give them a few minutes to collect their things and move clockwise to the next station, while I sang out loud, "Time to cha-a-a-ange stations/We must cha-a-a-ange stations/ Time to cha-a-a-ange stations/ A-a-a-again." They would always laugh at my singing. What a plan. Score a victory for my little daughter's brilliant idea.

At the end of the six projects, each group had bonded, and though adjustments had to be made where students were too disruptive, all in all, they loved it. After stations, we would come together as a whole class and go over *all* of the assignments, correcting each other's papers. The essay-writing station would require writing about a movie that we would watch together before beginning the station process. The movie was always a movie of substance, one they would not have seen. There are so many movies that have topics relevant to self-discovery and current topics of depth and complexity: Think of it. Homelessness, drug abuse, homosexuality, immigration, revenge, climate change, the entire panoply of human endeavor and drama can be found in quality movies. The movie can be timed to be seen as a reward for having finished and graded all of the work. Doing a literary analysis of the screenplay first, they write about the theme for their essays. I, of course, would read the essays and score them, providing feedback.

At the music and art station, they all listened to the same

music at a listening station, while looking at art books, making something creative on the theme of the movie, or writing poetry about the art or the movie.

One of the biggest advantages of having the students work around in groups is that the faster students can have free time and have access to things to do while the others are catching up. The challenge for the teacher is to organize the groups well and to provide helpful activities that lend themselves well to twenty minutes to a half hour times. Marking the stations by big numbers and placing the assignment on the wall under the number makes it so easy in the daily execution. Teachers can then take the time to sit with and work with the groups that struggle the most and take time to chat with and encourage further challenges for the groups that finish ahead of time. Then the larger projects can take as much time as the class needs. They ask me, "When is this due?" and I tell them, "When we are finished."

Chapter 8. Righteous Anger

There are instances when anger is the appropriate response. However, I try to remind students that, as in the words of Chris Rock from the video "No Sex in the Champagne Room," Young Black men—if you go to a movie theater and someone steps on your foot, let it *sliiiiiiide./* Why spend the next twenty years in jail/ 'Cause someone smudged your Puma?

This story is about some righteous anger that didn't do anybody any good.

Worst class scenario—two sections, ninety minutes each, with two groups of ninth-graders deemed unlikely to succeed. One class of regular English II in between. Tough schedule. The only saving grace that year was fewer students meant fewer essays to grade. But the exchange wasn't worth it. I had experienced success with self-contained classes of poor-performing students before, but they just weren't the mean little brats that these kids were. The students in these classes were mean to each other, and they were mean to me. And made the colossal mistake of being mean to my aide.

One day I put my little purse in my locking file cabinet, as was usual, but I didn't lock the lock. I stepped into the computer lab next door for a few moments to grab some paper, and when I returned, the purse was gone. It had 120 dollars in it. And of course, my wallet had my driver's license and credit cards, so I was really mad. But naturally, nobody "saw nothing." I *never* want to involve police in these matters, but I did call it in to the office. I told the associate principal I would try to find out for myself before involving police. I took the students out one by one and asked them if they had seen anything. The first day, no one had. But when the next day I pleaded with some of the good girls to tell me what they had seen, two of them, without knowing the other had talked, told me they had seen the boy named Jason grab it out of the drawer, pass it off to another boy, who passed it to a third boy, Sam, who sneaked it outside and came back in. They must have been quick; I will give them that.

Since both girls told the same story (and by the way, they were really sweet girls trapped in a bad class), I was convinced. I offered a thirty-dollar reward and no questions asked if anyone would bring it back. Then I took Jason, the kid who grabbed it first, into a room, and asked him if he took it home—I even called his home and asked his parents to look for it. They couldn't find it. He flatly denied having taken it but told me he would try to talk the other boys into bringing it back tomorrow for the reward. The next day, Jason brought the wallet back with the 120 dollars missing. (Of course, I had already called the bank about the stolen credit cards.) He then *had the nerve* to ask me for the reward! I laughed so loud I thought I would choke! "You took my money—split three ways you each have forty dollars, and now you want a *reward*? You must think I'm *crazy*! You ought to be locked up, but I gave you a break, and *that's* how you act?" I laughed in his face: "You're out of your mind. *And* I *want* my forty dollars back!"

My aide had been watching me try to deal with this extremely rebellious class for the whole semester. He was mad on my behalf. We used to joke around—once I said, under my breath, "Geeze, let's just get our friends and beat up the whole class." To which he laughed and replied, "Mrs. Demerson... we don't need our friends." That really made me laugh and put it all into perspective. They were small freshman kids, after all. But then one thief made my aide just a little *too* mad. And my evil prophecy came true. I learned to regret those words, even though I had been joking at the time.

We already know the boy in question, Sam, is a thief. One day he stole my aide's Jordans, which as you probably know, are extremely expensive basketball shoes. My aide was filled with righteous anger. But so far, he had handled his anger pretty well. Then he did something that surprised me in its maturity. He saw Sam wearing the shoes. At the time, they were walking past each other right in front of the main office. My aide, a senior, said to the freshman Sam, "Those *my* shoes!" And he grabbed the associate principal and said, "That kid stole my shoes, and he's wearin' 'em right now!" So the associate principal, who knew my aide because she was a basketball fan, took him at his word and called them both into the office. My aide told her to call Sam's mom and ask her what size shoe he wore, because clearly, they were way too big for him! So she did, and it turned out he wore three sizes smaller than the shoes he was wearing at the time. While she was making the phone call, my aide told Sam that he would tell the office he had *loaned* them to him, so he wouldn't get into trouble! What a magnanimous gesture – and he got his shoes back. I wish that were the end of the story.

As it turned out, no good deed goes unpunished. Sam actually walked from the gym one day and as he came towards my aide, pulled up his t-shirt and threatened, saying, "You want some of this?"

Well, that was the last straw. My aide promptly beat him severely, unfortunately breaking his jaw and putting a dent in his chest. The kid ended up in the hospital, and his parents threatened to prosecute for assault and battery. I think someone from the school somehow convinced them not to press charges, but my aide was the one who lost out in the end. He was suspended for a week and lost his basketball scholarship. His anger was righteous. Three strikes, Sam was out. But my aide got the worse end of the deal.

The boys didn't stop there, either. They stole an orange off of my desk and were openly eating it in the back of the room. Since I was known for giving food away very liberally when kids needed it, this really got to me. I remembered how my husband had told me to tell him who stole my purse, but I knew that would be a bad idea. But when I saw those kids eating my orange, I snapped and said, "You know, I love my profession, and I can't do anything right now because I would lose my credential. [Pause] But *let* my husband catch you out in the street!" The threat was very thinly veiled. Maybe it wasn't even veiled. Hell, I didn't care. After I had told them that if they needed anything, they could come to me, they stole anyway.

More about Stealing

The very first day I arrived at my new position at Yerba Buena High School where I transferred from the continuation school, a kid stole my pager. That kind of sets the adventure in time, since who uses pagers anymore. It was 1995. Four kids from separate classes came to tell me who had done it! He had been bragging about it out on campus and showing it around. I did give him a chance to give it back with no repercussions, but he didn't take advantage of that opportunity. Later I had the same kid assigned to my sixth period class and had to put up with him all over again. I acted as though nothing had happened and gave him a fresh slate, trying to ignore his smirking face. But even later, when I saw him working at my local Walgreen's drugstore, I went to the manager and told him he had hired a thief. Still later, I saw him working in my Wells Fargo *Bank*! I told the manager there about the incident as well, and immediately moved my account to another branch. Young people need only atone for their bad deeds by coming clean. If they don't, someone like me might extend the long arm of disapproval into their future in the community!

The converse is also true. Every student who ever returned something stolen with confession was promptly forgiven, and I encouraged all the other students to do the same. Even during the last semester of my career, two friends were able to reconcile when I talked one of them into returning a stolen electronic device and making full confession and reparation. They even shed a few tears as they realized they had done the right thing.

I had very good luck with having stolen or lost items returned to me. When my iPod was stolen—twice—I just said, "I'm not gonna sweat it. I will just buy another one. But you know who you are, you little brat, and I hope you are happy."

The cohesion in the social order was almost always in my favor: more kids found me trustworthy and were honorable themselves than not. I would help me find thieves, they would confess, they would return items, and they would often apologize so profusely it was almost embarrassing. I believe it was in part due to the fact that I kept free instant oatmeal and a microwave for their use, and often gave away Nutella on toast or peanut butter sandwiches. Kids steal when they are hungry, that's for sure. Get a bunch of granola bars and some Cup o' Noodles and keep them in the cupboard.

One student I had early in my career was so hungry every day, I would send him out on the porch to eat an orange before class. He was in a very low-achieving class and was not, at first, a very good reader. His reading began to improve, but his home situation worsened. I found out he had been living with his sister and her husband (he had no parents), but they didn't think they could afford him anymore, so he joined the Job Corps, the organization JFK started to help youths get trained for a job while able to live in quarters at the organization and have their meals there as well. The student managed to graduate a semester ahead of his class and got accepted into San José State University. He came by to visit and tell me his great news. I asked him what he would say was the secret to his success.

He said, "You know, Mrs. Demerson, tell them I never read much, but I watch *World News Tonight* every single night."

That alone (and maybe the food) made this student aware

enough of the world around him to become successful.

Make sure that if you give money, you always give privately at a break or lunch or after school. People have pride. When you hear a kid has run away and is broke and homeless, your twenty dollars given will come back to you many times over. Maybe not in cash, although every kid I loaned money to paid me back without exception, but the reward you receive is a sense of shared humanity. Priceless.

From a letter I wrote to my daughter, when her phone was stolen in the school where she had her first certificated teaching job:

Seeking punishment is not necessarily the way to go. I used to lecture all my students by looking them in the eyes and saying, "I want you all to learn this from the bottom of my heart and mind and soul. I really, really don't want you to steal because when you do, you are demonstrating to yourself and others that you actually have a serious character flaw. This is something that goes deeper than just a teen prank, it is something that will follow you through your life and make it more and more difficult to look at yourself in the mirror and say, 'I am O.K. I am a good person, and I have done the best that I can today. I am not asking myself for perfection, just a simple thing of saying that I didn't intentionally hurt anybody today. I didn't make the world a little worse today or make anybody sorry that they know me. I did the best I could.' This is how we grow ourselves from the inside out. This is what I want for all of you—I don't want the stolen item—I want you to grow your own beautiful character from the inside out. Because you are worthwhile, and you must believe that you can be a good person. If you continue to steal, talk to someone, and get some help. If you can't talk to your friends or family or me, find someone. Because stealing is a character flaw in the making, and you are still young enough to help yourself become better." This actually made a lot of students write me notes, after I told them to take out binder paper and write what they were thinking. It made me feel a whole lot better. I didn't get the money back that time, but I think a lot of kids were thinking more seriously about what stealing really means. Hope this helps.

It is good to remember they are still not *quite* adults and are therefore capable of that change in character that we foster, appreciate, and even marvel at when we see it. Witnessing change and reconciliation are the most beautiful gifts to those who work with the young. If you go into this career remembering that the "content of character" is the overriding goal: you will need to fight for it, model it, never give up on it, because no fight was ever more worthy.

Chapter 9. Sociopathy

Most disgusting examples of sociopathic behavior [Who does this?], and the consequences I brought to bear:

> 1.   Student claiming he would "rape an underage pussy.": Immediate expulsion from summer school
> 2.   Student who looked like a 30-year-old, with mustache and leering face, grabbing my velvet jacket pocket right at near private level and saying, "That feels good." Immediate permanent suspension from my class
> 3.   Student who, when I shook his hand on the first day of class, stated, "That's the hand I jack off with." Immediate suspension from my class and immediate transfer to a male teacher's class

Are you shocked? Because in the middle school class where my daughter taught in Brooklyn, a kid told her, "Lick my ball sweat."

These are the kinds of things we have to endure until we don't. A teacher must put a metaphorical foot square in the rear end of any student who tries this incredibly disgusting behavior. If we don't get support from discipline staff on these kinds of things, what does that say to the rest of the students? That it's OK to demean, to denigrate, to insult, to vilify, to horribly dehumanize and even to threaten teachers, who woke up with nothing more on their minds than to figure out a new way to help students learn. What other occupation asks you to plan each day, persistently, for edifying and aiding other human beings—

who confront you all day, persistently, with resistance, insults, and even threats? Why do we do it?

As I told my students, "If there is only *one kid* in here with the sincere desire to learn something today, *I am here for that kid.* And the rest of you, by damn, will *stay out of the way so learning can take place.* I am responsible for *this* learning environment, and I take my responsibility very seriously."

I am so grateful that the vast majority of kids are interested in learning, and in fact, I would say only about four percent on any given day are serious behavior problems. One bad apple doesn't spoil the whole bunch, but five can. Learning to sequester, separate, and quarantine the "bad actors" is a skill one can spend an entire career trying to learn. But the ones that want to learn are always worth the work.

How can we tell if a student has no conscience, or has a dangerously impaired character? It won't be difficult. The problem is the student cannot be appealed to through normal means. I have had students who were mentally ill. They may have many problems, but not be devoid of conscience. The students who show blatant disregard are frightening. I had one gangster student whose name appeared on my roll sheet for most of the year, yet he had never appeared in class. One day he appeared looking too old for high school. Teachers in the English office had told me that before I came to work at Overfelt, they had a lot of big students who were "dangerous with a capital *D*." There had been a riot in the street on Cunningham Avenue, where many were injured, and many police responded. This student seemed to have come from that era. I could not figure out why he had been kept on my roll yet never appeared, so I asked him to come up and sit by my desk, so I could quietly interview him while the other students were working on that day's assignment. He said he was MIA because he had been locked up. I asked him what he did to get locked up. He told me the following story:

"I was living in Stockton at the time. I went to a 7-11 with my girlfriend, and some guy hit my girl with a carton of cigarettes. So I threatened him, and he said to meet him back there at three o'clock to settle it. So I came back at three to the vacant lot across from the store, and I had my shotgun, and he had his shotgun, but I fired first. I tried to hit him in the legs, but I hit him in the chest, and he died. He was wanted by the police for a bunch of shotgun killings, so they gave me about five minutes in jail, and now I'm out."

What the hell? I had just witnessed a student confess to murder. I kept my act together throughout the rest of the day, but when I got to the babysitter's to pick up my daughters on the way home, my knees gave out and I collapsed to a chair. I must have been going on adrenaline until all my responsibilities were completed, but then the sudden drop in that chemistry boost turned me into a rag doll. The next day I asked the other teachers about this kid. They showed me a newspaper article that confirmed what had happened. He had indeed received a very short sentence for such a heinous crime. And then as the class adjusted to having Marshall in there, some of the girls started to like him. He was actually trying to be personable, but I never trusted him for a minute. One day he came in during my third period class because he wasn't getting the requisite C in my class in order to make the basketball team. He held up his arm like he had a gun pointed at my head and said, "I want my grade check. And it better have what I need, or umma come back and punch you."

I told him, "Marshall, I will work the numbers on break, and if they add up, you will get your C." At break the C did not compute. So I went to the commons room and in front of all of his friends I told him, "Marshall, I'm sorry, the numbers just did not add up." *What was I thinking? I just told a murderer that I wasn't going to comply with his threat!*

His response: "That's OK, Mrs. Demerson. I probably wasn't

gonna make it anyway." Whew. Again, still not sure whether or not I should have been afraid.

The next episode in the adventure—Marshall gets arrested for going to a local bar with his shotgun and robbing it. He put the money in the back of a *gold Cadillac* and drove over to a neighborhood house and parked outside. The police followed the bartender's description and arrested Marshall inside the house with the gold Caddy parked outside with the shotgun still in the trunk (duh). He was taken to adult jail because he had turned eighteen. One day during that sixth period class time, he called me from Elmwood Correctional Facility! He said he just "missed" my class. The girls were saying they thought he was cool. I asked him on the phone why he did it. He said he thought it would be fun.

I said, "Are you having fun now, Marshall?"

"No."

"The girls in the class think you are cool, but I told them you are *not* cool."

He said, "You tell them you are right, Mrs. Demerson, because this is *not cool*."

Later the school gave Marshall a forum to speak to aspiring gang members, ostensibly to warn them away from criminal life. My husband was so offended by this because as he says, "Why not ask someone to speak who *never* gave in to gang life? Someone like me who had to fight to stay *out* of the gangs." I hear my husband's voice in my mind as I address these issues. His experience and wisdom have steered my course in teaching on so many occasions and has given me a perspective that is rare and precious to me. And I say to all my students, I know what a fifteen-year-old is capable of. Because my husband at fifteen lived in a house no bigger than this classroom with eleven brothers and sisters and had no time or space to do homework, so he got a forty-hour-a-week hard labor job, moved into his own apartment, bought his own food, made it through high school, and got good enough grades to play on the football team and run track! If he can do all that, I know you are capable of a lot more than you think. And no excuses for shortcuts.

But these admonishments mean nothing to a true sociopath. I had another student admit he had been locked up for a hit-and-run. He said he was glad, that he would do it again. He didn't last long in school. But he would return to campus with his pit bull on a chain, and walk around in the back toward the end of the school day, trying to look intimidating. I always called security immediately.

I had a student stay after class during the Obama campaign, walk up the middle aisle to within a couple of feet from my face, and say to me with a fierce, Twilight-Zone look in his eyes, "You know Obama is the Devil." My diagnosis is not one of a professional psychiatrist, but I referred that student to the office as a serious risk. He threatened to come to my house and mow down the whole house. In his particular case, I scheduled a meeting with the associate principal and the student advisor, because one can never be too careful. The student advisor agreed with me after having spoken with the student a few times himself. The boy's affect was off, and his laugh was decidedly sinister. This was a student who needed to be watched very carefully.

I warned the boys that hung around with him to be wary of his mental instability. One of them came to me later and admitted he had let that boy drive him across the city, and the boy had sped down the freeway at a hundred miles an hour, scaring the life out of him. He told me, "I didn't believe you at first, Mrs. Demerson, but man, now I see what you mean!"

The next story illustrates the difference between a sociopath and a psychopath. Although I am not a psychiatrist, to me the difference is the delusional mindset of the schizophrenic child in contrast to the cold calculating super-rational sociopath. I was teaching a boy who seemed odd but not necessarily of any concern to me, other than the fact that he was extremely quiet, kept to himself, and painted his fingernails black. Some "goth" kids were doing that, so I wasn't too concerned at first. But one day after a long absence, he came to the door of my classroom, stood just outside, and asked me to come out to speak with him. I got the other students busy and went to speak with him. Here is what he told me:

"Mrs. Demerson, I couldn't come to class because I was locked up at (local hospital mental ward). They had me in there for seventy-two-hour observation because I have a list. I have a list of people I plan on killing. And Friday I shot at one of the girls on the list, but I missed, and they took me to the mental hospital. I want to go back because I feel out of control."

!!!! My first reaction: "Am I on the list?"

"No, Mrs. Demerson, but I have about seven more people on the list that I am planning to kill [mumbled something about Marine Corps]. And I want to feel in control, but I feel out of control. So do you have any books I could read and do a book report on for credit for your class?"

!!!! My next reaction: "Well, yes, Reynaldo, I can give you some books for when you go back to the hospital. Let's find something that's maybe science or something, not like the book you did your last book report on, though." (*World's Most Famous Serial Killers.*)

He left with his books, and I called the main office and got a hold of the counseling associate principal, who told me something about, "Oh yeah, Mrs. Demerson, we know."

And I said something about, "Well he needs to be picked up and taken back to the hospital right away!"

And the AP said something about "Oh yeah, of course, and if you see him again just let us know."

And I said something like: "*See him again*!? Aren't you going to pick him up right now?"

It seemed as though their reaction was completely disproportional to the danger of having a boy walking around with a hit list. Again I made it through the rest of the day, but when I got home to the babysitter's, my knees went out from under me and I collapsed. At least I wasn't on the list. Delusional young person who was considerate enough to warn us.

Remain calm. Remain calm. Remain calm. Remain calm.

Chapter 10. Mean Girl Syndrome

Isn't there a TV show called *Mean Girls?* Or is it *Gossip Girls?* I have had enough of both, in my own years of school and in my classrooms. I don't want to watch them on TV. Mean girls are not allowed. If girls are mean to each other, it is as though the gender that was blessed with more equanimity and more innate nurturing tendencies has turned on itself. I can't see why anyone would let mean girls bully any more than they would let boys do it. It is their passive-aggressive stealth mode that is most destructive. Sometimes we teachers do not see the psychological stabbing these girls are getting away with. When we do, it is imperative to find a way to work with these mean girls to keep them functioning in the learning mode and keep them from the damaging crimes they are capable of. Because they are hurting themselves as they hurt others.

It helped me to remember that each mean girl had a story. In one last period class I had a girl who gave me grief every day. For some reason, she was just going to argue with every single thing I said. She was sullen and never cracked a smile. I tried to treat her with equanimity, but she really tried my patience. One day towards the end of class, she was up turning in a paper. She turned to me and said, "Mrs. Demerson, it's just been me and my dad for two years and I have to do all the housework and everything. But today, my mom is coming home from prison." Do I need to describe how much it rewards a teacher to be patient?

In another class, four girls were tittering and laughing, getting attention from other students while making faces and commenting about a boy who sat near them. He was an older boy who seemed mature, yet he would do odd things. He became angry and insisted that I was being overbearing when teaching about women authors; that I was not being fair when I used their work and insisted that the students present a book report about a biography of a woman. I would do this because no one else was doing it. Women are still left out of most of our history lessons. After an entire class presented oral reports on women, the students often commented that they learned more than they thought they would; and that they now recognize how few women they even considered as important to history before. I explained to this adamant young man that indeed he was correct: that I was going to focus for this part of the class on women writers. I explained that it was only for part of the class, and that he would live through it, despite his outcries. He later apologized profusely and told me he understood my choice and respected the perspective he gained. Somewhere during our conversations, he confided that he had not been raised by his parents since he was very young. He was one of those rare children who virtually parented himself. And not just because he lived in a dysfunctional household. He lived in *no* household. Kicked out and abandoned at the age of twelve, Alfonso came from Mexico to the United States by himself. He was a street kid who was one fast learner. Intellectually, I place him in the top group with only four or five other students I have known over the years.

The mean girls were always overreacting to his odd comments. I struggled to keep my temper in check every time they started in on him. But I realized they were completely surprised in an unpleasant way by his being "different." Once he told me he had been rejected by a girl out on brunch break in the quad area. I asked him what had happened. He told me that he went up to her and "I just told her, I want to be your friend." The girl and her friends laughed at him. What they did not realize was that street children and others not parented from a young age simply do not learn the same socialization patterns in which other children are well-schooled.

In my life, I have been the victim of those mean girl looks, those mean girl laughing bouts, and those mean girl outright insults. As a teacher, I was in a position to change the climate of the room. Let us be clear. The problem wasn't Alfonso. The problem was the girls' thinking that they could have a free pass for their rudeness because he was odd.

After some particularly disruptive insulting chit-chatting, I waited until Alfonso was out of the room. Then I told those girls I was sending them out to be fixed, since they were the broken part. They were aghast. I called the female student advisor and told her that the girls should be counseled and warned about rude behavior. When the four of them came back, I took them out of the classroom and explained that Alfonso had an extremely good reason for his inability to act according to their circumscribed world view, and that they really needed to dig deep and demonstrate more character. We never had a problem after that. I never told Alfonso what exactly had been done, but his days were a little easier. We must persist in our beliefs in the power of change. Certainly I felt better about the climate in the classroom, and I knew that the girls would feel better about themselves as well.

"Tonight the mirror will forgive my face."[4]

[4] Alexie, Sherman, and Jess Walter. *The Lone Ranger and Tonto Fistfight in Heaven.* 20th anniversary edition. New York: Grove Press, 2013. Print.

Chapter 11. Fight Club

I couldn't decide whether to laugh or cry the first time I visited the campus where I would begin my credentialed teaching career. As I was escorted by an English Department Chairperson down a wide sidewalk to the English Office, our attention was arrested by a fantastical scene. A girl with a blonde ponytail in jeans and a T-shirt scuffled energetically with *two* Cambodian boys, and she was winning! She had one under each arm and she was somehow slinging them around and intermittently smacking and kneeing them without mercy. It took two male staff members to pull them all apart! I thought to myself, *Wow, that was entertaining*. But crazy, right? As the fighters were hauled off to the office, I had very little time to wonder about their fate. I found out later that this girl was raised in a very hard neighborhood in New York City. Whatever had been her past experience, what in the world led to that fight? I was never to find out exactly, but I still wonder. Never saw anything like it before or after. It was like a weird window into Fight Club. I was to discover that just as my husband has pointed out, sometimes people enjoy fighting. It is not always a case of bullying.

For the most part, I have found that students don't usually want to fight, but the three most common reasons are: jealousy—one person talking smack about another person or their mama or best friend or girl- or boyfriend; or gang fighting, most often when sides have been chosen and gang members have identified themselves as "down for their color." As one *fifth generation Norteño* explained, this literally means they have pledged to fight and *kill* or die for their color. But another reason is general sporting, which I call Fight Club. When boys fight because the opposing baseball team has been unsporting, it is a free-for-all that some of the most well-brought-up boys engage in with abandon. Many report to me that if they had it to do over, they would, despite the consequences, because it was "hella fun," and the sense of camaraderie was exhilarating. So I gave up trying to fault them for that attitude as long as no serious injuries were incurred. Of course we don't condone it, but sometimes...

Girl fights are the worst, as any high school student can attest. I found out boys would not even try to break up fights between girls because "they fight dirty." Once I was shocked out of a lesson plan when suddenly two very large girls, one Samoan and one Mexican, threw over their desks and went at each other with hurricane fury. They were smashing each other around the room and hitting the wall of the portable classroom so hard the room was shaking as though a wrecking ball had hit. I yelled for the boys to help me break it up, but they said, *"Nooooo, Ah, hell no. Look what they're doing!"* I looked to find one girl yanking the pierced earring out of the other's ear straight through the skin. All I could do was yell, "Knock it off!" but they were way past hearing me. I had called the office for help, and when the discipline team arrived, both girls were hurt. I had to go back to the other students. When I went back inside the classroom, the kids tried to say they had tried to warn me trouble was brewing. I said, "What are you talking about? I didn't hear anybody say anything."

Then a couple of students said, "We went like this" – while rolling their eyes in the direction of where the girls had been sitting. Oh my goodness! How was I supposed to see that? That was *way* too subtle of a cue. But it is a testament to how little other students want to get involved in mess like that. I felt so shaken by seeing the girls hurt. I still wonder if I could have been more attuned to the temperature in the room.

Another time, a girl jumped out of a tree behind my classroom onto an unsuspecting victim below her and broke her victim's arm. When a girl had the temerity to let red bra straps show out of her white blouse, two *Sureñas* (girls from the gang who wear blue) jumped her right on the porch of my classroom as everyone was leaving class. I ran outside and chased one of them named Shorty down towards the creek in back of the school, and I caught up to her. I could have grabbed her by the hood of her sweatshirt and jerked her back, but at the speed we were going I would have hurt her, so I let her go, yelling, "Come back tomorrow and get expelled." So she did; and she did. One girl who loved to fight was from Richmond, a predominantly Black, impoverished and crime-ridden area around San Francisco Bay. Her older sister explained to me that the younger sister had been born infected with HIV from their mother, who had died young. I no longer wondered why she was so testy. Remember, HIV-AIDS was a death sentence in those days.

Another memorable, strange fight between two boys, one of whom was transgender, had its origins in that portable classroom. The boy named Jorge was an amateur boxer, training in a community boxing program. He was also a thief. The other student Miko, who identified as a boy but was biologically a girl. Almost all of the students in the class thought he was a boy, and everyone called Miko "him." I was to find out later that a few of the girls had gone to middle school with Miko, and knew he was biologically female because he took girl's P.E. class with them. On this odd day, Miko protested that his wallet had been stolen. Right during class. I made all the students stay in their seats and lectured them, but no one seemed willing to admit to the theft. I rewound the video in my head of what had transpired that day and remembered that Jorge had been the only one to leave the classroom, and that was only to go outside on the porch.

So a trusted student and I stepped outside and searched around. I remembered seeing Jorge jumping up outside on the porch. We looked on the roof of the little porch, and there was the wallet. We brought it in, and Jorge, confronted with the evidence after everyone else was allowed to leave, laughingly admitted he had done it, and said he was just goofing around. Later, at break, apparently Miko went up to Jorge on a little hill, and they got into a fight. As they were rolling around on the ground, with Miko actually beginning to *win* the fight, his T-shirt was pushed up, and the Ace bandages he used to bind his breasts were uncovered. Everyone who saw then knew about his birth gender, and knew that the thief, Jorge, was getting his butt kicked by a "girl." It was such good comeuppance that I must admit I felt the braggart wannabe boxer got what he had coming to him. But I don't think Jorge was a really bad person, as later he apologized, and things were resolved. I was proud that very few students reacted to Miko's outing. He went on as normal.

I have witnessed some gang fighting that was pretty outrageous. The worst was seeing a boy get his head kicked in, which triggered a seizure. I ran to my classroom to call the emergency number, shaking and feeling nauseated.

Conflict Resolution and Gang Intervention

We are always warned about gang intervention. It is not something I would choose to do if there were a choice. Sometimes there isn't. Once the kids wanted me to dress as a *chola* for Halloween. A *Sureña* girl (the one called Shorty) did my hair and makeup, and I wore huarache sandals, a *cholo* shirt, and chinos. I posed with several groups of students in the quad, later realizing that they were Black girls in one photo, Asians in another, Latinas in another, and white girls in a fourth. I was flashing four fingers on one hand and three on the other, so that the *quatorces* (14's for *Norteños*) and *terceros* (13's for *Sureños*) didn't get upset with me. One girl had drawn the four dots on my knuckles of one hand, and that was seen by some *Sureña* girls, who represent with 13 or 3. They put the word out at brunch that they planned to jump her. She was a white girl in special education, who swore she did not belong to a gang, and was only messing around. I had the girls all meet with me in the career center to have a talk. Before the white girl arrived, I took the other girls into confidence and told them that she struggled with learning and was not really aware of what she was doing. Shorty and her friends told the girl, "Hey this is serious. We don't play around with this. You were about to get your ass kicked at lunch." The girl denied over and over that she was serious, and the crisis was averted.

I never dressed as a *chola* again. It had been fun, the kids got a big kick out of it, but it wasn't worth running the risk of a misunderstanding. The makeup was so realistic, when I went home, my daughter, asleep on the couch, woke up and jumped three feet into the air, screaming, "Where are my parents!?" I had to speak calmly and reassure her, "It's Mom, Baby, it's Mom!"

I normally look like this:

Another time, two boys were about to get into it over gang affiliation. I quickly realized I was in over my head and called the counseling, health, and principal's offices, asking for someone to come in and do a gang intervention. No one arrived. I took one boy next door and the other stayed in the classroom – they were threatening each other, yelling back and forth. I closed the door and spoke to the one in the next room first, hearing his side of the squabble. It did appear that the other guy was at fault. Still no one arrived from the office. I went back into the classroom to speak with guy number two. I figured, well, this one is on me since the cavalry has not arrived. I spoke with guy #2, and he finally admitted there were concessions he could make. He didn't know what to say.

This is where I took a chance on using a tool that proved later to come in very useful in similar situations. I took some index cards and a pen. I asked guy #2 to tell me his thoughts. As he spoke, I wrote down what amounted to an apology, but framed from his own words. Then I told him, "Now, I trust you. Hold on just one more minute." Went back in to guy #1. Told him, "He's going to come in here, and I am going to leave the two of you alone. I am going out on a limb and trusting you to hear him out.

You may not leave until I have heard the outcome."

Guy #2 goes in, armed with a fallback plan of simply reading his cards. Situation resolved. Met both at the door; they agreed to stay away from each other and operate in class as though nothing had happened. The gang intervention people never did arrive. (Or maybe they were there all along?) At any rate, when a crisis is averted because students are given tools, we cannot help but feel a sense of accomplishment. I cannot recommend this strategy for a situation that is too hot, because we all know violence does not stop outside of schoolroom doors. But when we have a sense that there is a possibility for de-escalation, we must act as mediator to the best of our ability. It is a matter of modeling a cool head and having an expectation of the best.

Once a group of Vietnamese gangsters who had it in for somebody on our football team came to their practice with guns, threatening the players. As I walked down the sidewalk towards the gym foyer between the parking lot and the side of the gym, I was actually trapped between the gun-toters and the football team, who were running *toward* the armed kids, in full uniform. I don't know why exactly the armed boys were leaving. I watched, wild-eyed, backing up slowly, as they ran into the parking lot and jumped into a white minivan. They were yelling, "See you at Kennedy!" I got the license number of the minivan and wrote it down. As the campus police drove up in their little golf carts, I tried to get their attention, repeating over and over that I had the license plate and a description of the students with guns, but they simply were not listening to me! It was like a movie in slow motion. I couldn't get them to listen until about fifteen minutes later, when I felt as though they had missed valuable time to catch up to the armed students.

Eventually they did take my information, and I heard later that the campus police had gone to Kennedy, an elementary school across the street, and apprehended the gang boys. I heard from the football players later that they weren't scared, but I thought they should have been.

Who does that? Who runs *toward* gunmen? Adolescent males, apparently. And who listens to teachers? Not cops, apparently. I have never felt so invisible. In the case of not being seen by the gunmen, it was a blessing. In the case of not being heard by the police, it was frustrating. But nobody died that day, and I didn't even have to use my AK.

Chapter 12. Rapscallions

I don't have too much to say about rapscallions. We all know who they are. They are the ones who make homophobic comments. The ones who tell the teacher lies for no darned good reason. The ones who bug other people relentlessly just to be annoying. The ones who have to be told more than once to stop name-calling. The thing to remember is that for the sake of the group, call a jerk a jerk. Why should a jerk be allowed to continue being rude? I gave my students only three basic classroom rules and made them memorize them at the beginning of the year. They had a quiz on them. These were *my* non-negotiable rules.

#1. Never ask me if you can go to the restroom. You are a grown man or woman, and you do not ask another grown man or woman if you can use the restroom. Just write a pass, and I will sign it. *Do not talk to me about bathroom issues.*

#2. Never hand me papers. Put them in the basket. I have a mental block about papers handed to me into my hands. I lose them. I promise you, I will lose them. I just do not notice you have given me something. If you put them in the basket, my aides will organize them and keep them together with clips. These papers will not be lost. Ask the kid who handed me a twenty-page research paper. Two years later I found it in one of my laundry baskets at home. I have absolutely no idea how it got there. So I mean it. You must forgive me this weird brain glitch I have and save yourself a lot of heartache.

#3. Never get in anyone else's learning space. This covers every other contingency. Do not respect anyone who does not respect you, but you must behave as though you do, so that they are forced to rise to your level since you will not sink to theirs. So you will sometimes be asked to stay in a bubble where you will be seen by me, but do not reach out physically or verbally to others to disturb the learning process. Sometimes, such as when someone is reading aloud, you will be asked to be rocks. Do rocks move? Do they make any sounds? *No.*

We have a lot of fun talking about being in our learning bubbles or being rocks, acting it out. Funny to hear kids saying, "Mrs. D, she's getting in my bubble!"

When students can't follow these three rules, they are jerks. Let's not waste much time getting them to stop. *Be firm. Say, "No".* Say, "I understand, but *no*."*

The one time I was truly frightened in class happened in the Opportunity Program. I had ordered pizza to be delivered to the class as a reward. I learned that day that hungry teenagers can very suddenly present a mob mentality. As I was being swarmed by students who were being egged on by a mean little rapscallion of a boy, I realized for the first and only time: *I am not in control of this situation.* I was literally pinned to my desk as they angrily grabbed and gobbled. It took my breath away. If there hadn't been enough pizza, I felt as though they might have actually attacked me. The culture of the classroom that day was reduced to animalistic behavior. Luckily, the food calmed the beast. I was quite unnerved. That same boy once threatened me: "I'm going to have my mom come and drag you out." I grabbed the phone and pretended to look up her number."

OK, let's call her right now and invite her over. I would like to tell her what you are saying about her." Enough is enough. He shut up and left. Thus it was like the Twilight Zone when later, my husband and I took our girls to Chucky Cheese pizza place for kids, and this particular boy served us very politely and even offered our daughters extra balloons. I was aghast at his turnaround in behavior.

¿Quién sabe?

Chapter 13. Well-Meaning Annoyers

Sometimes students are just annoying without meaning to be. This may be due to ignorance or bad smells. This may be because they just don't quite believe they *are* annoying. It may be that they have never learned not to be creepy to girls. It is up to the teacher to model sophisticated behavior and to sometimes give actual lessons in what Doctor Montessori called Grace and Courtesy.

Once a year I hold a Teddy Bear Picnic. At this picnic, by invitation only to one class and sometimes other individuals, we have a day when students can bring a stuffed animal to class. If they bring the stuffed animal and behave courteously, they receive twenty points to substitute for one homework assignment or quiz of twenty-point value. I set it up with several little tea sets on tables covered with white paper. We bring only the kinds of food teddy bears love, like Trix, Fruit Loops, Colored Goldfish, or frosted animal cookies. Students must first introduce their stuffed friends, then themselves, as we go around in a circle listening politely. Then the tea party goodies are served. If a student chooses not to participate, that's fine. I'm happy to say that rarely does anyone want to abstain. If they do not have a stuffed animal, they can sign up ahead of time to borrow one of mine. I also have a Cambodian Barbie doll they can borrow, or a Korean 12-inch doll, gifts from Cambodian and Korean students. There are special tiny cups for them. They must give the toys their tea before they can have cereal and tea themselves. It is a memorable day of good behavior, and one that models trust and appropriate social interaction. We also play the

Teddy Bear Picnic song, and dancing is not frowned upon.

You might think high school students would not want to be so silly. You would be wrong. "High school students are just fifth-graders in disguise" (learned from a wildly entertaining science teacher at a Bay Area Writing Project workshop). Regressing to a safer time is sometimes quite therapeutic for all of us. And taking cell phone pictures of a grown boy soccer player feeding a Barbie doll a tiny cup of tea can come in handy for extortion later. "If you don't (insert appropriate desired outcome here), I'll just show the pictures to the team!" I say, laughing insidiously, but winking. I actually make sure it can be seen by the team by messaging it to another player. I cannot recommend that every teacher do this, but I can emphasize the importance of taking time out for Grace and Courtesy.

How to cope with well-meaning annoyers: Put on your most compassionate face and have that uncomfortable chat. Do it when you have the student alone at a time when no one notices you have that student sequestered. Tell him or her about the problem honestly and with great tact. Do not allow yourself to respond to their denials with any elevation of emotion. Keep it simple and offer your help to create solutions. Make sure you let them know that you as a team can solve the problem together, and that they will not be singled out for criticism if you see that the offender is working to improve the situation. But be firm. If you hear any more complaints about the problem, then you will be having a different conversation. Sometimes, as in the case with body odor or inappropriate annoying clothing, referral to a same-gender advisor is a good idea. The idea is not discipline; it is to lower the stress in the learning environment. Who wants to sit next to a stinky? What girl wants to have to look at some boy's gluteal separation in the seat in front of her? Who wants to hear someone honking into a Kleenex sounding all slobbery? Ah, Bartleby. Ah, humanity.

I witnessed outrageously annoying behavior that is so funny

to think about now, but completely shocking at the time. One girl in my class kept acting rowdy and silly. She surprised other students with her ignorant outbursts. One day as I heard gasps and Oh My God's, I looked up to see that she was turned away towards the back of the class, straddling her chair in an odd position and yelling some rock and roll mantras – she turned slightly in profile and I caught a glimpse of what was causing the gasps. She had her jeans zipper pulled down and was starting to pull down her pants! I squealed her name and *"What the hell are you doing?"* Amidst the subsequent laughter and chatter, I called the office and told them to send a liaison to remove her from class immediately. No one seemed to know why she had done that!

Some time later, I saw her with her mother in the local grocery store. Her mother was squealing about something in a wild manner, and her gestures were flighty—her arms flailing around in circles as she alternately complained and giggled about some goofy grocery adventure. I thought to myself, well, the apple doesn't fall far from the tree, and then I started to laugh myself silly until I got to my car. Even now the picture of that girl in her half-dressed exhibition makes me giggle, because it wasn't salacious, it was simply outrageous.

My student teacher had a class where student behavior went beyond ridiculous. The kids had no attention span and no filters, and they did no work. We'd hold it in until after class, but then we'd laugh until our guts felt about to burst. One kid, a kind of overweight, lazy boy, used to drive us crazy. He never stopped poking other kids, saying completely nonsensical things during a lesson, never turning in work, and had one memorable behavior that I still laugh at to this day. The student teacher, Huma Saleem, who was gifted and sweet and a born teacher, was giving a lesson about being from a neighborhood where life is difficult, being able to escape to a better place, yet never forgetting where you came from. It paralleled the wonderful story the class was reading by Sandra Cisneros called *House on*

Mango Street. Huma showed a video with the same theme, called "Jenny from the Block," by Jennifer Lopez. That kid kept saying "I'm Jenny from the block," drawing out the last word, every single time he saw her, every day, every fifteen minutes or so. There was just no stopping his mocking. We tried. He sounded ridiculous even to his peers, but he just would not stop. After class Huma and I would stare at each other and burst out yelling: "I'm Jenny from the block!" until our sides split. She learned that laughing at these kids is sometimes the survival technique to make it through another day. She told me she wouldn't have made it through without the ability to share those laughs. Later she taught community college remedial English, in which versions of these types of kids arrived just one year older, and the perspective on laughing at them after class contributed to her ability to cope there as well. I mean, "I'm Jenny from the *Block!*"

Another time there was a boy in my last period class who was a constant, ubiquitous annoyer. I got along with him fine if he had plenty of tasks to do at all times, but when he had the slightest amount of down time, he would start a ruckus. A roly-poly freshman, he was class clown in a most irritating array of behaviors. Whenever I could no longer continue class with him in it, I would send him to the office with the appropriate written referral. Once I asked the associate principal if she would like to keep him as an office aide. (She didn't think that was funny.) One day as I headed past the class to open the door to the computer lab, in came an associate principal to have a little chat with me. He asked me, with boss-challenge voice, why I always referred this boy to the office. Just then, right on cue, I heard a hubbub in the classroom. I turned just in time to see this boy pulling off his tear-away basketball warm-up pants, standing in the middle of the room in his plaid boxer shorts! I tapped the administrator on the arm, pointed in through the window, and squealed, "See! *That's* why! That's *why!*" That picture spoke a thousand words. The administrator whisked him away to the office, quite convinced of my concerns. He was obviously to be suspended from my class for at least two days. But a few days later, an advisor saw me in the parking lot and asked me if I wanted to take him back. It was the end of a long day. "*Hell,* no!" I exclaimed. "You must be kidding!"

"Mrs. Demerson! You sound worse than the students!" she scolded. But I never saw him again.

Chapter 14. Pets

Although it is never a good idea to spoil one child over another, teachers are human beings, and some day, a particular student will make an inroad into a place in your heart where you cannot deny you have a pet. I remember my first pet student as though it were yesterday. Wendy Perez was the cutest little freshman girl, with enough charm that all the boys would fall at her feet. I remember her coming into class early before first period to plug in her blow-dryer and put on the finishing touches just before class began. I cannot tell you how that endeared me to her. She seemed to think of my class as her home. Once she told me that she would rather bring a sleeping bag and stay under my desk for the weekend than go home. Little by little her story emerged. She and her mom just couldn't get along. It wasn't unusual for Latino parents to be protective. But her mom was *just* a bit extreme. Wendy wasn't supposed to date, wasn't allowed to have a boyfriend, but of course, she did. She was constantly in fear of getting caught.

Apparently, her mom added insult to injury when she got into trouble at home. I couldn't imagine anyone insulting this beautiful, cheerful sprite of a girl. Wendy used to help me with everything. When my younger daughter turned six, Wendy even came to the house to help me set up for the party. We were decorating in all purple. I had balloons to put up, and I asked Wendy to put six on the door in the kitchen. She kept saying she put six, and I kept saying "That's not six!" She finally in her exasperation with me took me by the arm, pulled me a bit away from the door, and made me look again. With a sweep of the arm, she demonstrated the six. She had formed the *shape* of a 6 in balloons on the door. It took more than six balloons to do it. We laughed until we collapsed. That was the kind of relationship we had. Our older daughter, Spirit, loved Wendy because Wendy could do an impersonation of Madonna that was completely spot on. At eight, Spirit was a complete Madonna fan, and she and Wendy would compare stacking bracelets and fingerless gloves, Madonna boots, and off-the-shoulder tank tops over contrasting color tank tops underneath—oh, the fashions and dances of the '80's. In class, Wendy could be counted upon as a welcome distraction. Right in the middle of a lesson I might find her standing in the aisle taking off a shoe to see if she could get the heel back on. She had no concept of that's not being OK. Because she would give me a huge smile and a wink, I had no choice but to laugh and give her quick, but never severe, admonishment to behave. Once I looked up, and there in her big brown eyes, I felt a connection that was electric and indescribable. I felt I was seeing myself.

Wendy took my lessons to heart. She said she hated to read. When I found books that were at her level that had high interest for her, she suddenly began to read voraciously. I always feel that there is a book for every kid, we just have to find that book. She wanted to know how to improve. I gave her some simple advice that has been the key through the ages. Find a book that is just a little bit hard to read, look up the words you don't know, and then just read more. The more you read, the faster you read, the more you enjoy reading. Period. But it has to be something you are interested in, at least until you are a really good reader, who can read really fast over the parts you don't like. Wendy took off like gangbusters. Years and years later, my boss, a new associate principal, told me he remembered me when I taught at Overfelt High School. He had been one of those freshman boys who came around to my class to moon over Wendy Perez.

Wendy's family came to the U.S. from Mexico and had lived in a studio apartment with four kids. They worked cleaning other people's homes and managed to raise some of the sweetest kids who ever lived. Wendy's brother Johnny, who was also in my class, was a year older, but behind academically because he had early health problems. His parents had to take him to Mexico, at great risk of not being able to return, in order for him to have heart surgery. He made it, and they made it back. He was even on the cross-country team. One day a driver on some kind of medication jumped the curb on the street behind the school and plowed into several boys on the team. In front of Johnny's eyes, one boy was catapulted into the air and died. It was an event of such horror: Johnny spent the entire night screaming and punching the walls.

These children's lives were a window to levels of drama I had not seen before. We often search for spiritual answers when the unanswerable happens. Why do bad things happen to good people? As my husband pointed out, what is more important is, what do good people do when bad things happen to them? Wendy became a Registered Nurse. From a second-grade reading level as a freshman to a four-year college degree, I would say Wendy was more than a pet. She became the example I was to cite for many struggling readers for years to come.

Sometimes students, just as adults do, become your friends because you think on the same wavelength. I have had students who shared my exact love for music or shared my level of intellectual curiosity and attitude about a certain subject. When you connect with students through music and literature, it is much easier to find you have made friends that are lasting. The respect you may have for some students and they for you will put you into a mutual admiration society. This is different from the students whom you like just because they are kids. I actually like kids an awful lot unless they are just horrible. I often wonder how teachers get into teaching who don't seem to like kids. They like to pressure them, to denigrate, to "cut them down to size." What they miss is the huge bag of photographs like the one I have of students who wrote loving things on the back.

Many of their names I don't remember, but seeing their faces in their graduation pic, or their prom pic, or their sports team pic, and I remember the "them" of them. And I can only tell new teachers that the human beings you meet are going to change you. Let them in.

Chapter 15. Funny People

Some kids in class are just so funny that never a day goes by where you don't feel the wings of joy lifting you above the day-to-day. Who wouldn't laugh at someone who can cut up, get into trouble, laugh and go to stand outside, then hold the door frame, swing in and yell, "But I lo-o-ove you!" Oh, my goodness! You just want to bust a gut laughing. The faces kids make can get the teacher going. Just as a student who makes a mean face all period long can drive you crazy, one who makes a silly face when they think they might be in trouble can almost erase the offense. I hope the students who are thinking this might work for them are not reading this book. But I honestly can *not* stay mad at a kid with a grand sense of humor.

During my last few years of teaching, I began to take a few notes of the funny things kids would say or do. I wish I would have had time to do it all along my career, but there would probably have been no teaching going, on because classes were a laugh a minute so much of the time. I know there were a lot of challenges, but somehow, I remember more moments of fun than pain.

Here are some of the notes I took and the funny kids who inspired me:

Funny kid #1 – Justin. Okay, Justin gets in the book for the oddest behavior. Justin would make my life strangely miserable during regular class time by insulting me outright. Once a group of my former freshman honors students took a path though my classroom to get to the computer lab. I always welcomed friendly interruption no matter what the lesson, because, after all, no lesson is so damned important that happiness doesn't come first. The kids were waving to me and saying, "Hi," so I was waving and saying, "Hi!" enthusiastically back at them.

Justin interrupts loudly, with a scowl and a growl, "Don't pretend you're popular."

The class was aghast, and someone said, "Whoa, why do you let him talk to you like that?"

There was no way I could have explained to the class why I let Justin insult me on a regular basis. But this is why: Justin was a very slight, short, smart, articulate Filipino former gang member. He was a complete contradiction. He would put on a mean front all day, then come after school unbidden and do my typing for me. He typed *ninety* words per minute. He told me about his life and how he was working to help his family. All this work he did for me was so incredibly needed and appreciated. So I didn't react when he did his tough-guy routine in class. And my rewards were worth it. I still have some of the voluminous documents he typed for my curricula. And a friend who would never admit to being capable of such caring.

Funny kid #2 – Martin. Martin interrupted every lesson with stories from his life that were so compellingly funny or fascinating that the lesson had to stop. Then we were off track, and we would have to start all over again. He often gave money to homeless guys in the streets of East San José. He never hesitated to help someone in need, which meant expending lots of extra energy. And he worked almost full time as well. He had no papers as his family entered illegally from Mexico when he was little. When he was able to get a job at a 7-11 convenience store, he told me this heartening story. The 7-11 was always being robbed. But when Martin started working there, those same homeless guys he had helped came to him and told him, "We got your back cuz you had ours. We won't steal from you and we won't let anyone else do it, either." (Pause for joy.) Martin used to make fun of everything and laugh at everything. He was such a merry soul. We still address each other as Mart-i-i-i-n and Mrs. Demer-s-o-o-o-n because of a brilliant actress' lines in a Tyler Perry movie (Byr-a-a-a-n!). One day he interrupted class again as we were talking about military recruitment. He told us the recruiters kept calling him incessantly. Then finally he just told them, "I don't have my papers," and "They left me alone after that!" He told this with such unabashed glee that the class burst into laughter.

When so-called "illegals" feel comfortable enough to share their status in your class, you can feel that you have created the safe environment children need. When they can be funny about it, they have an intrinsic safe place in their hearts where they can generate something real and joyous to share with others who face similar challenges. Laughter is not only the best medicine; it is also the best protection when the selfish predators are circling. Laughter is sanctuary.

Funny kids on ghetto life: One year a book came out titled *You Know You're Ghetto When...* It was a picture book of things that a family might have around the house if they were "ghetto." So Rainy called me from a friend's house to tell me about the book, and said, "Mom, We're on *every page!*" Laughing, thank goodness, at our silly plight of not having enough extra money to fix up stuff around the house. And not really caring, since our priorities were met, such as dance lessons and modeling classes and lots of books. As I recall, one of the pages read, "You know you're ghetto when... you have the lid to the toilet sitting on the floor in the corner in the bathroom." Check. "You know you're ghetto when... your sliding glass door handle is made of duct tape." Check. And so on.

I decided to ask some of the students what they would put in a book if we called it *Ghetto Family Stories.* Then I gave my examples of crazy stuff we had around the house, like another one from the book where "You know you're ghetto when... you can't fully open your front door because your furniture won't really fit in your living room." Check.

The kids really got into the spirit of the thing when I put on the board:

"Ya, We G-H-E-T-T-O. Getting a Higher Education To Teach Others."

One student contributed several well-told stories. One was about an older Asian woman in his neighborhood who went outside every day with an umbrella, rain or shine. She was always in the process of painting her house. She would paint a big swath down the front, say four feet wide, then change her mind about the color. Then she would try another color for a swath a few more feet wide. Not exactly the same width, though. Then she would apparently change her mind again, until the front of the house was some bizarre unintentional rainbow, with colors not represented in the rainbows of the sky. We laughed about this, all the while knowing that she was probably mentally ill, but bearing her no ill will, so the image in our brains was just plain funny. Another of that student's tales was the time his mom was having friends over for a lovely tea or coffee party around her table. Dad had been working in the attic where the ceiling material was thin, and suddenly her husband's boot-clad foot and leg came crashing in from the ceiling! Plaster and drywall rained down on the tea party, embarrassing the mom. As my student had been up there with him, this was hilarious to him, but I don't think his mom thought it was so funny. Alas, she didn't have any more such get-togethers for a while. You know you're ghetto when... The next story he told was probably the best one to exemplify the genre. He had friends who used duct tape to repair their *microwave oven*. You know you ghetto when, you got duct tape on yo *microwave*. Combining the shabby with the dangerous, yet surviving equals humor. (See section called *Drug Use and Other Missteps*).

As the stories came in, they became funnier and funnier, and I finally shared this one: We had painted our older daughter's room a pleasant blue. One day when she was home alone, she lit a candle and fell asleep. The candle was next to a poster, which caught on fire. This caught a tapestry on fire that was behind the poster. The tapestry caught the wall on fire. She slept through the whole thing, but somehow, the fire put itself out. (I like to think a guardian angel came through the window, and her wings gently blew out the flame.) The damage behind the poster and tapestry was that the paint just heated up and bubbled away from the wall, leaving brown to black scarring and brown bubbles. Here's the ghetto part. Our punk-rocker daughter took a can of brown spray paint and painted the word "feces" next to the big brown bubbles. Indeed it did seem an apropos caption. We left it there until she moved out. Then instead of scraping the wall properly and re-painting, I just took a blue sheet and used a staple gun to staple it over the mess, put up more posters, and turned her room into my office. You know you're ghetto when... (It stayed like that until she was in her late twenties, and brought her loved one home to visit, in preparation for which we finally re-painted properly.)

After telling this story to my students, they came forward with many, many more. My little disclosure prompted a big response, because I humbled myself to let the students know that I'd had hard times too, but emerged laughing at myself.

There is an art to Ghetto Family Stories. They have to be funny. They have to be born from poverty. They have to be reparable when better times come along. There we have a formula. One family just didn't get the concept, which made it even funnier to me. Oh my goodness. A lovely Fijian Indian girl told me excitedly, as she did everything excitedly, "Mrs. Demerson, I have a Ghetto Family Story for you!" I asked her to go on. "One time we cleaned our patio sliding glass window. And then our dog ran straight into it!" Uh... no. First Principle met: it was funny to picture the dog smashing into the door. Second Principle *not* met. No hint of poverty in the story. (You are *not* ghetto when...)

So her brother came in later, and I laughingly explained how his sister hadn't really understood the concept, and I told him about their dog story. He told me excitedly, as he, *also,* did everything excitedly, "Mrs. Demerson, Oh! Oh! I know one! Our dad cleaned his car in the driveway once, and, ya, he used old rags from a box in the garage!"

Uh...no. Dad has a car, and he cleans it. Like most everyone in suburbia. Apparently, this family, although they had plenty of serious troubles in their lives, just did not know ghetto. I am glad for them, but their misses in the "You know you're ghetto when..." category were huge. They make the book as examples of what *not* to share when you share Ghetto Family Stories.

You know you're ghetto when... You ask your class: "How many of you have an uncle on *Fugitive Watch*? (local program showcasing felons sought by police)," and a third of the students raise their hands. Then you all burst out laughing because there are so many, yet here the kids are in school, at least trying to G.H.E.T.T.O.

Chapter 16. Electronic Devices

I think we can safely say that personal electronic devices are the ones we must ignore. Cell phones are often funny, they aren't often dangerous, and teachers make way too much fuss over them. If you can't beat 'em, join 'em. Again, it's about proportion. As I said to the class while on the phone with another teacher, "Hey you guys, I don't interrupt you while you're on *your* phones! Don't interrupt me on mine!" The teacher on the other end couldn't stop laughing.

Verdict: "We are Borg. *Resistance Is Futile.*"

Use electronic savvy to your advantage at all times. Stay current with social media. A friend in need is a friend indeed, and an Instagram friend is a friend in need. These kids need connection. They are reaching out. Are we going to be on the other end? There are ways to keep what is private appropriately hidden from kids. A little common sense goes a long way. My daughter's boyfriend asked me at my retirement dinner what I was going to do with my time. I answered that I did plan to keep up with friends and students via Facebook. I had recently posted advice to some students who had expressed suicidal ideations on their Facebook status. (These days it's Tik Tok, and soon it will be something else.) I said I hoped it had helped. Later in the evening he asked, "So... what will you be doing when you're not saving lives on Facebook?" Charming.

When Common Sense Took a Vacation

I had a student I will call Daniel. He was in a class that my beloved student teacher was working with as an English One student. He was a very, very attentive student and earned a good grade. But it was a class filled with English language learners. The next year he was summarily advanced to English III when the principal decided all the juniors would go to what would now be Junior English whether they were prepared or not. *The Scarlet Letter* and *Beloved* were completely unintelligible to him. He wasn't ready, but continued in his good-natured way, to try to learn. Despite a failing grade, he smiled and let me know he would be making up the credits in a summer school or after school program. He brought a friend, Ruby, from last year's class to visit during lunch. It was all good.

Year three comes along. Daniel is now a senior and is again in my class, this time to prepare him for the CAHSEE, the California High School Exit Exam required for graduation. Daniel was getting an A in the class. But his behavior had radically changed. He was now disruptive, often using his smartphone to entertain the girls around him. I tried changing the seating arrangement, but it didn't seem to work, since pretty much everybody in that class was disruptive. I told them to put the phones away if they were going to disturb the lesson with their use. One day I had had it. No lesson was going forward because the students would not stop talking, fidgeting, yelling across the room, turning around in their seats, or getting up to use the trash can or get a Kleenex or *show someone else a video*! Oh my goodness! This was my last year of teaching and the nonsense was just as much chaos as my first year. I saw Daniel turn around one more time with that damned phone, and I snapped. I went over and when he wasn't paying attention, I grabbed the phone off of his desk and took it to mine. A student teacher was behind the desks on her side a few feet away. Daniel followed close on my heels yelling, "Mrs. Demerson, give me my phone!" To my shock and dismay, he grabbed my wrists and twisted them until he got the phone out of my hands. I sent him out saying, "You must go to the office—that just earned you a referral. That could be an assault charge. Go see Mr. R."

I should not have resisted. I was beat at that game. Don't take on a challenge you can't win. Let the discipline team handle it. Here I was a thirty-four-year veteran, and I violated a common-sense principle. I felt defeated and sad that our friendship had been shattered.

I did not want to let that incident go, because my wrist actually hurt, and it just wasn't something that can be easily forgotten. I followed through with a call to the advisor and was told I must contact a parent. (They always tell you that, but I usually ignore it—I find my time is better spent moving on, forgiving and forgetting.) Knowing that the parents did not speak very much English, I called the older brother around 2:00. He was at work, but promised he would call the mom and that she would come to school. I told him I did not think it urgent enough for her to come right away. At 3:05 I got a call that she was already there.

I went to the office and met up with her, waiting with her and her young daughter, who spoke excellent English. The little girl translated my explanation and concern to her mom. I stressed that Daniel had been one of my favorite students in the past, and that I was shocked and disappointed and didn't know what was going on with him. I was hoping she could shed some light for me. The little girl said that he had been changing his behavior. They didn't seem to know why either. We waited. Awkward.

In the office, I told Mr. R. that Daniel had been sent to his office the day before. Daniel yelled at me angrily that he *had* gone to Mr. R., and that he had given him detention. Mr. R. was quite upset by this because Daniel had not come to see him at all. Apparently, someone else had given him detention, but for another problem. Now he had compounded the problem by lying. In the office, Daniel flat denied that he had twisted my wrists. *He even said he had witnesses* in the class who would back him up! I explained that they couldn't be witnesses because they were on the wrong side of the desk and could not have seen, while the student teacher was my witness who was on the side where it happened. The conversation was being translated into Spanish for the mom by Mr. R. I understood enough to know that he was doing an excellent job.

Mr. R. stated that we seemed to be at an impasse. Did I want to take it to the next level and involve the associate principal and the police? No, I did not. I wanted to get through to the old Daniel. Where had he gone?

The conversation became emotionally charged. The mother insisted that she believed her son. I made a plea to say that what he had done was no reflection on her parenting, that I knew she was a good mom. I urged Daniel to tell the truth. He accused me of getting him in trouble when it was the students behind him who had been badgering him. I apologized for having missed that, but insisted that his track record led me to believe he had been disrupting others. So many times I had asked him to put that phone away. Not because it was a phone, but because he was making the girls fall over with laughter, enjoying their attention. All perfectly understandable for a young man, but unacceptable in the middle of lessons. I reminded him of the times I had allowed him to step outside and regain some equilibrium instead of getting in trouble. Again he insisted it was I who had been in the wrong. Again Mr. R. said we would report incident up the chain to the principal and/or police. I looked at Mr. R. and said clearly, "*No.* We're not through here."

Mr. R. asked the mom about Daniel and explained that he knew him to be a hardworking boy. I concurred. His mom explained that he had been working at a job and giving his money to the family. We were all starting to feel emotionally overwrought.

I took my last shot, praying that it would work. *"Daniel. I know you want to be a good man.* Do you want to be a real man? A man like my husband, who, because he is Black, has had to stand up and face so many, many bad things in his life. *But through it all he never lies!* He just keeps his head up and takes the consequences no matter what they are! Daniel, you *hurt* me! I went home and told my daughters what you did. I cried because, Daniel, *I am your friend*! I am not your enemy!

We were all crying. I was sobbing great sobs when he looked into my eyes and said, "I'm *sorry*, Mrs. Demerson. I am your friend, too."

We all hugged. I told Daniel I would see him tomorrow. He said, sniffling, "See you tomorrow, Mrs. Demerson."

The next day Mr. R. called me in class and quietly said, "Man, Mrs. Demerson. I have been in a lot of parent teacher meetings, but no one has *ever* made me cry before."

Thirty-four years, about to leave the profession, and this small save took me to a level of intensity that made me say to myself, *"They will make you know what it was to be a teacher. They will take your very best at the very last. You don't get to rest. You need to remember."*

Daniel passed his California High School Exit Exam.

Chapter 17. The Purpose for/Bane of Our Existence: Teen Love

a.) *Gag Me with a Spoon*

b.) *Most Beautiful Thing You'll Ever Witness*

c.) *Relationship Violence*

a.) *Gag Me with a Spoon*

Whenever I think of teen love, I think of the boy who had to excuse himself from his final exam. I went outside to find him crying his heart out because his girlfriend had just dumped him. I felt so sorry for him, but I just kept thinking, *bad timing!* Because of the breakup, it was extremely likely that he wouldn't do well on his exams, and that would probably have a more long-lasting effect than losing the girlfriend. But teen love is undeniable. Every year during our study of *Romeo and Juliet*, I assigned the Honors freshmen the job of debating Teen Love is Real: True, or False? They debated in teams during class, and then wrote their papers. Every year they ended up getting very excited to debate the issue, and often left the room still arguing.

Is it possible to truly love someone at such a young age? My favorite responses included the notion that love is quite difficult to define; therefore, how can adults judge that the love teens are feeling is not real love?

One girl wrote: "The excited feeling you get when you touch, or the nervousness you feel with the first kiss, or the pain you feel when an important relationship ends is the same whether you're seventeen, twenty-seven, or fifty-seven."

I cannot dispute that their feelings are real, even though from my vantage point I know that they are probably neither lasting nor mature. Yet isn't it love? If one truly tries to put the other's personal growth ahead of the stifling possessiveness that cripples so many romances, isn't that true love? I try to stress that, when a romance ends, young people should attempt to remain friends, and to build on what good did come out of getting to know each other well.

I noticed a student who was quite devastated that her boyfriend was breaking up with her. He was younger and a bit more "bad boy" than I thought she deserved, so I wasn't truly unhappy about it, but she was miserable. He told me he was angry with her because she hadn't been "there for him" when his brother was going to jail. She separately told me the same thing.

I looked at her and these words just popped out of my mouth: "Are you afraid to talk with him about it because someone in your family is locked up, too?"

She burst into tears. Sobbing as I wrapped my arms around her, she said, "My Dad. We never get to see him." It was obvious she couldn't handle the overload of emotions when her boyfriend tried to tell her about his brother. She told me, "Thank you for being like a mother to me, my second mother."

That touched me deeply. I don't know how I guessed what was going on with her; it was as though somehow all the years of being around young people in crisis had given me a window into the heart of the matter. When next I saw the two of them together, I gently suggested that they talk about it so that they could remain the very best kind of friends: those who have something deeply personal and painful in common and can therefore help one another and show that special empathy. It was clear he was still too angry to forgive what he considered a betrayal or a let-down at his most vulnerable time, but they did agree to remain friends.

One principal recommended that we acknowledge that *everyone* has the right to want to love and be loved in return. To deny this very compelling urge is to deny what adolescence is—to deny what being human is.

Sometimes the gooeyness of teen love is just yucky. Everybody gets tired of those kids who can't do anything without their boyfriend or girlfriend. The hearts and flowers and balloons and candy can really go over the top.

The sexual aspect especially during young adulthood is very strong, of course, and one cannot ignore outrageous PDAs (public displays of affection) when one is the adult in a school environment. But affection is one thing, and overt sexuality is another. Kissing until hickies are all over the neck while at school is a bit over the top. Wrapping bodies around each other gets to be too much. But sometimes a little sitting with arms around each other and sneaking smooches isn't so bad. I think adults are envious that they don't get to do that! I used to walk by couples standing on the sidewalk kissing and say, "She doesn't like *you*," really loudly until they would have to break apart laughing. But I actually loved seeing the smile in the corner of some kid's mouth when they would spy their girlfriend or boyfriend approaching, and I used to think it was quite sweet when they would send notes or gifts, even though that could become a brief distraction in class. I could never help but feel cheered to see someone kiss their loved one a quick goodbye before running off to separate classes. How could one blame the teenager for wanting to do something demonstrative? Don't we all remember wishing we had someone to care for us?

I often set up a lesson for evaluation, asking teenagers to establish their list of criteria for a good potential mate on the left-hand side of the paper, and to establish evidence on the right-hand side if the person they are dating or would like to date meets those criteria. I ask the boys first and we put the criteria down the left on the overhead projector for all to see.

It often surprises the girls that they don't just focus on looks. The guys want intelligence and sense of humor, honor, loyalty, and good conversation, just as the girls do. Then when they pick a girl they are thinking of, they have to show proof that she actually demonstrates those qualities. It helps us all to think about what is truly important in a life partner. It is also a great tool for learning to evaluate, which is clearly a skill most do not fully develop, as evidenced by the fact that they do not take the time to create clear criteria and seek concrete proof. It is a lesson for writing that helps students to flesh out their ideas. As a life tool, we can see that finding a partner is not easy. It is my hope that young people give thought to these things as they seek their future love. But as we all know, when love enters the building, often logic goes out the window. *Romeo and Juliet* is such a great vehicle to discuss the complete idiocy of passionate, irrational love. Dead bodies are not the goal.

I was just looking at a darling picture on Facebook of a baby in a Halloween costume. I shared the picture with my daughters, explaining proudly that I had taught both the mother and the father in class some years back. They were a sweet couple then and are making a great family now. It is rather rare that teen love evolves into adult fidelity, but it does certainly happen. In communities where extended family is considered extremely important, and the larger the better, one sees more examples of these young couples creating lasting relationships.

On the dark side, however, teen intimacy is fertile ground (no pun intended) for so many risks. The risks of loving and losing are high. I often would see a girl come into a classroom crying with just a certain look, and I would quietly ask her, "What did he do?" I would not even know the girl was in a relationship, but she would say, "How did you know?" and I would say, "Do you want me to kick his ass for you?" This usually brought a bit of a smile, but often she would need to go outside and collect herself, usually with a girlfriend along.

But don't get me started on teen "love" poetry. I'm glad they try to express themselves with words; I am an English teacher, after all. But...Gag me with a spoon.

b.) Most Beautiful Thing You'll Ever Witness

The best of all possible scenarios for me was to witness the many examples of sibling or friend love that I was blessed to have seen. When I arrived at Yerba Buena High School in 1983 for my second phase of student teaching, I was assigned to an English class that met in the band room. As I stood in the back surveying the room, I was startled to see two Latina girls sitting side by side, one with her arm over the other's shoulder, stroking and playing with the other girl's long, beautiful braid. I was so surprised by this because in my high school, no one would have dreamed of sitting so close to one another, and we certainly wouldn't have touched during class! It was a gesture intimate, yet so very friendly and, I imagined, soothing, that I went from feeling surprised to feeling happy in the space of a few seconds. The kids told me that, in Mexico, kids often walk arm in arm with the same gender, and they bring their familiarity and affectionate ways with them when they come to school here. My friend who taught pre-literate students even had two boys who sat in the same desk together. The other students had no surprised reactions whatsoever, simply affectionately dubbing them "*los cuates*," colloquial for "the twins," or "the close friends." One vision will stay with me forever as the exemplar of the goodness of kids and the reaffirmation of my belief in their potential. As I approached my classroom door, I saw one of my boy students jumping up onto the back of another boy, hugging him and tousling his hair, and all the while falling apart, laughing, proudly beaming. "He's my brother."

c.) Relationship Violence

It seems that teen relationships are at the basis of most fights in school. And there is always plenty of he said/ she said to go around, stirring up the already-active adolescent imagination and energies. I admit I used to get amused reading the updates one of our principals would email us, describing the supposed reasons kids were fighting each other, often citing trash-talking about one another over a boy or a girl in a "love triangle." The way he described them, even without names, we most often knew who they were.

As adults in a school environment, we have to take relationship violence very seriously. From https://www.dosomething.org/facts/11-facts-about-teen-dating-violence,

> "1. Roughly 1.5 million high school boys and girls in the U.S. admit to being intentionally hit or physically harmed in the last year by someone they are romantically involved with.
> 2. Teens who suffer dating abuse are subject to long-term consequences like alcoholism, eating disorders, promiscuity, thoughts of suicide, and violent behavior."

Often the signs that one student is abusing another are not obvious. I have put off writing about this because it so deeply saddens me to think about the microcosm of a school. It is a world within the larger world of society, and it makes one think about all the ways in which we hurt one another. And each and every case is different. Schools try to make policies, but there is never a one-size-fits-all approach to working with human beings.

As I once told our principal, "I am a woman first, a mother

second, and a teacher third. And I will always see the student as a person first from the perspective of a mother; that is who I am."

So when I saw kids in crisis, I didn't think about policy, I thought about kids. I made mistakes. But I was fully there and present as much as I could be as an aide to their emotional as well as mental well-being.

Once a dark-eyed beauty in my junior class came into the room and sat at her desk normally, and as others filed in, I noticed nothing unusual. But a young man whom I did not recognize strode in, walked to her desk and the radar went off. The tone he was using with her set off alarms not only to me but to some of the boys in the class who remained standing as she was telling him to leave and leave her alone. I marched to her side and squared off with him and told him he was to leave the room immediately. As soon as he left, I asked her what was going on, and she explained that he was her baby's father and was not supposed to be coming to school as he did not attend there. I asked the boys if two of them would escort her to the office to report the incident while I called ahead to ask for security and to alert the office. A girl student came to my desk and told me that she had seen the boy earlier on campus and he had a gun and had threatened her to tell him where his baby's mother was. She said she had told him that she didn't know, and he was asking other people as well. I got nervous and called the office back, requesting an all-out search for this guy, explaining about the gun.

A short time later I was sent a substitute and told to come to the childcare center as they had apprehended the guy, and since the legal offense of coming on campus without leave and making threats was witnessed by me, I would have to place him under citizen's arrest. As I walked into the center, I looked into an office to see the most frightened face I had ever seen. The boy was handcuffed to a chair, looking up at me with pure terror on his face. I felt sickened and didn't want to do it. They told me I had to read it out loud. "I hereby place you under citizen's arrest." I read the complaint form and signed it. I didn't quite understand that protocol, but I knew I was willing to see to it that he was stopped. I still wonder why I was asked to do it that way. I saw the girl in a different part of the building, asked her if she were OK, and she said yes, that her parents were coming to take her and the baby home, and that they would swear out a protective order against him.

Why did she have to go through that? Emotions run so strong where sexual relationships are involved. That is the reason why I advise students not to get involved sexually at such a young age. I have never believed that it is immoral, but rather that it is much more emotionally fraught with dangers than any young person can possibly anticipate before these consequences come into effect. Adults are rarely prepared for the emotional fallout. Youth are *never* prepared. That is why we must continue to keep the legal age of consent higher and try our best to guide young people to find fulfillment in the many things life has to offer that are not about sex. Certainly more easily said than done.

In one of my last years of teaching, I taught a young lady who was not a particularly good student, though certainly a good-natured and lovely one. I used to tease her and her boyfriend as they sat on the bench outside my classroom, hugging and playing together. He was one of those kids who looked much older than he was, with a beard and kind of a gangster look, but they were always smiling at me as I teased them. They would want to linger together after the bell, but I would shoo him away and tell her to come in to class. The next year, he was in my last period class, and she had moved on to another teacher, but still they sat outside my room on the bench and hugged and played, and just generally seemed quite happy and content. As I realized he had learning disabilities and did not attend class very often, I wasn't surprised, but I continued to bug them both to try to get him to come to class. I asked them the usual questions about what their plans were for after high school, and he always said, sure, he was going to go on to college, but I began to think he probably wouldn't. She seemed to have at least a little more on the ball academically, and I was hoping she would receive good guidance senior year and try for more education. One thing was for sure; they were inseparable.

One day the teacher next door to me, a new, young teacher whom I had befriended, asked me in to her room to speak with one of her students. To my dismay, the student said she had seen that boy slamming the girl into the brick wall of the bathroom building. I was so glad the young teacher had come to me, knowing that I knew those kids and wondering what she should do. She asked me if she should report it, and I asked her to allow me to look into it first.

I found the two in the back parking-lot, and thus began the most heart-wrenching conversation of my teaching career. I told them what I had heard, not telling who had told me. I did not leave room for them to argue, even though she started to protest that he did not hurt her. He tried quite feebly to say that he did not abuse her, but the looks on their faces told the whole story. They could see how differently I was acting, looking deeply into their eyes and maintaining an intense tone of voice. I told them that I had watched them for three years. I told them that from what I had seen of their relationship, they loved one another. I told them that I had really enjoyed watching them take care of each other and be so happy in each other's company.

Then it was time to talk to him. "You have no idea what you are risking. You have a beautiful young woman by your side who is like a beautiful flower. And she will defend you because that's what we do. We don't want anyone to know about our pain because it is deeply humiliating and makes us feel like *shit*. And she may even continue to love you. And she may even stay with you for the next twenty years. But look at her now! (The tears began to flow from all of us.) She is so beautiful and trusting! If you continue to hurt her, she may stay, but you will be damaging her forever! And one day you will look at her and realize that she is not the same *person! You* will have changed her forever and she will no longer be that beautiful trusting flower that you have beside you right now! You must *promise* me that you will never lay a hand on her again! Because if I ever hear any reports again like I heard today, I will do *everything within my power* to see that she gets away from you, and you will never see her again!" The looks on both of their faces were so incredibly sad. I hugged them both and said, "I love you both, and I want the best for you."

They said, "We love you, too."

We all cried. We walked away in silence. It was completely draining. And I was so close to retirement. I thought to myself, again: *these kids are asking the very best from you at the very end.* I went home so tired, but somehow feeling that if one is to make a difference, then all the stops must be pulled out. And one must risk laying it all out on the line with complete honesty and give these young human beings the very best, the very deepest, the very hardest lessons from the heart of the matter.

Part II

The Making of a Teacher

I give all this background information because I do not think one can assess a writer's motives without knowing something of his early development. His subject matter will be determined by the age he lives in — at least this is true in tumultuous, revolutionary ages like our own — but before he ever begins to write he will have acquired an emotional attitude from which he will never completely escape. It is his job, no doubt, to discipline his temperament and avoid getting stuck at some immature stage, in some perverse mood; but if he escapes from his early influences altogether, he will have killed his impulse to write...

Using the word 'political' in the widest possible sense. Desire to push the world in a certain direction, to alter other peoples' idea of the kind of society that they should strive after. Once again, no book is genuinely free from political bias. The opinion that art should have nothing to do with politics is itself a political attitude. [iv]

I was born in a high Rocky Mountain valley on the border of Wyoming and Idaho, where the cowboying is real. Snow falls at least ten months of the year. One joke goes like this: What is a Star Valley summer? Two weeks of bad sledding.

The early settlers came with the Great Mormon Migration. Mother's grandfather was one of those early settlers with plural wives and many children. Like those early setter families, there were eleven kids in Mother's family. Grandma, a feisty little red-headed Irish woman, came west from Pennsylvania and married my grandpa, whose first wife had left him a widower with six children She then had five more, of whom my mom was oldest. Perhaps that's what prompted her to become a teacher. She had plenty of practice with her younger brothers, while her mother was busy in a time when all laundry was done by hand. They had no electricity, no car – only a buckboard wagon and a team of horses.

Grandpa had a huge vocabulary, and my mom thought he made up a lot of his words, like "pusillanimous" and "obstreperous." Later when she read more of the dictionary, she was pleasantly surprised to find out they were real words. Grandma made sure each and every one of the eleven Hepworth children received at least a bachelor's degree. This was quite an accomplishment for a poor ranching family. My mother skipped two grades in school and went off to Salt Lake City in a cattle truck to begin attending The University of Utah at the age of seventeen. She asked the truck driver, "May I sit in front, or do I ride in the back with the rest of the heifers?" (I love what my daughters call Wyoming Humor – they don't love it quite as much.) She became a teacher at twenty, and she was the best I have ever seen.

Mother taught Latin and English for thirty-seven years. I would leave elementary school each afternoon and walk over to her high school, where she would let me sit in a desk and watch as she put declensions of Latin in colored chalk on the blackboard. She ran a tight ship, filled it with love and intellectual honesty, and students loved her. When she went to a new high school later, there had been only two foreign languages taught there previously: French and Spanish. By the time she had been there two years, over half the students enrolled in foreign language chose Latin! We still enjoy looking at photos of us at the Latin Club's yearly banquets, where Mom dressed as Juno and Dad as Jupiter. My brother, in his turn, got to be Apollo and my sister went as Minerva. I was allowed to attend either as Hebe, handmaiden to the Vestal Virgins, or Cupid; in the latter case I held bow with rubber darts for arrows at the teenage girls and boys I thought would be a good couple. (I'm sure this was disconcerting for some and just maybe fun for others.) I walked from Vandalia Elementary to Vandalia High School every day after we little kids got out and watched her last classes. She and I would walk hand in hand through the halls, and my heart was filled with the joy of her love.

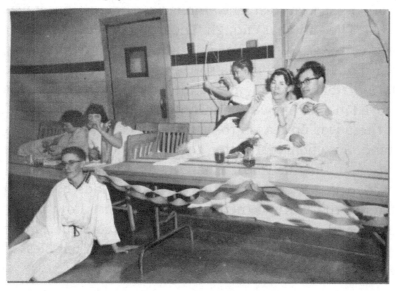

I learned the art of teaching from the best. It was always difficult to see other teachers without comparing them to her – and of course, they were bound to fall short.

Mom was a loving and extremely feminist woman who taught her daughters and son humanist values. Both my parents were devout atheists, and their kindness and dedication to intellectual and personal honesty gave me a great start. I was their third child, and by the time I came along, they figured they pretty much had the parenting thing down pat. They were quite relaxed and lenient with me; their other two children were turning out well and I seemed like a trustworthy sort.

I only lied outright to my mom twice in my life, and I found out it just wasn't worth it. Once Mom had bought some special chocolate-covered cherries for her mother who was in a nursing home and was saving them for when we would see her next. She put them up high, above the refrigerator, probably thinking "out of sight: out of mind" for us. I sneaked in and ate a few at a time, several times. When Mom found out, she asked me if I had taken the chocolates. I lied—she spanked me really hard and reminded me how selfish I had been to take my little old grandmother's special treat, and emphasized how serious it was to lie to her. The guilt was enough. The next time I deceived her as a seventeen-year-old, I stayed out until four in the morning, and when I got home, she was so frantic that I could see the potential horrible effect of my actions on the person in this world I loved most. That was a lightning insight. Mom reminded me that there was no reason to lie to her, as she would always understand. So when years later I was reminded by students just how much they lie to their parents as a matter of course, I was saddened. I wanted to think that most kids could tell their parents the truth. When I discovered just how harsh, judgmental, and shaming some of their parents could be, I more carefully considered my judgments of their lying. I felt blessed to have been trusted.

Mom and Me

Mom was teaching in Star Valley when we had to move to Ohio. Dad was an aircraft mechanic, and the work had petered out. We moved back to his home state of Ohio, and later to Indianapolis for the same reason. But even if there had been work, the pressures of being the only non-Mormon nuclear family were getting a bit wearisome – the LDS church was the only show in town. There were only 120 people in our town. What social life would be in store for us there? Much as we missed the beauty of Wyoming later, there really was no choice for us.

It was my early adventures in literacy and my love of grammar that put me on the path to teaching English. Mom always read to us with joy and enchantment, and there were books everywhere. I learned to write "Hannah Lynn" at around four years old while standing over a big black round kitchen stool. I remember clearly how happy I was to see the wonderful shapes and learn that they were sound symbols that "meant" *me*! At five years old I was reading *The Black Stallion*, by Walter Farley. I remember reading it, I remember loving the glossy cover paper with the stallion rising up on his hind legs, black against red. I remember the story, but what I don't remember is having to bother to learn to read. Later I came to understand that my mother had given me that gift by an instinctive knowledge of what Dr. Montessori called the sensitive period. The period when the brain is most ready to learn symbolic language is age four, and missing that period actually delays reading as one becomes less absorbent each year afterward. It has been my experience that educators often wait until six when two years have been missed, thinking children too young for sounding out. My mother knew things from mother-wit, and from a highly perspicacious intellect.

She often told us, "There's just no substitute for brains." Or phonics.

Cigarettes and Poison Ivy--My School Years

I had a unique kindergarten experience as well. The class was taught by a Native American woman who held kindergarten in her own sprawling home, which she had fit with teeter totters in the basement conversion, and a huge garden in back complete with poison ivy. She taught us to skip from rock to stump, trusting us not to jump in the ivy. We did wonderful worksheets of arithmetic and I remember lots of praise. Mrs. Mench was marvelous. She was a beautiful, tall woman with a long, low, black ponytail, wisps of grey around her temples – and she spoke in a deep-throated articulate and patient voice. I would see her step outside to converse with my mom while enjoying a cigarette. She wore long, fifties-era skirts, black, with her own brightly-colored hand-painted designs. I still have one of those cherished skirts that my mom bought from her and wore for years before I did. Later those skirts made parts of costumes for my daughters, so a little of Mrs. Mench's art lives on. My appreciation of brown-skinned people began there as well, and I find it fascinating that she was the only one I met for so many, many years afterward.

In Vandalia, Ohio, there were two elementary schools for all of us little white middle-class kids. Mommy bought me the book from Vandalia Elementary because I would be going to Woodleigh, and Woodleigh would start with a different book. I enjoyed it but went through it in a few short minutes. Alas, on the first week of school, I was transferred to the Vandalia Elementary, and was faced with having to read the book I had already finished. Oh lordy, the boredom. Fortunately, my teacher, Mrs. Routley, recognized and relieved my distress by giving me options to read pretty much anything I wanted. Thus I joined the ranks of dinosaur-o-philes! I had a little friend, Walter Rumbarger the Third, (yeesh), and we devoured anything and everything there was to read on the topic, setting up little dinosaur scenes all over the tables in school. Mrs. Routely was my first lady crush, because she treated us with respect, was little and cute, and had a husband who was in a wheelchair, which we found noble and dramatic. It *was* noble and dramatic. Bless Mrs. Routely; I will always love her.

But the gift of literacy was not appreciated equally by everyone, I was to discover to my dismay. When I was six, Mom was teaching me grammar, and I was loving it. As I went about my chore to put away folded laundry, she was giving me doses of indirect objects. "He gave *her* flowers." I never forgot. Spelling came easily for me, and I absorbed it like a Shamwow. I honestly loved the language and loved where reading could take me so much that I couldn't imagine how a teacher could try to stomp that out.

Apparently my second-grade teacher was attempting to do just that. Her name, aptly, was Mrs. Storment. Placed into three reading groups, called Blue Birds, Red Birds, and Yellow Birds, we were well aware of which group we were in, and why. Later as a teacher myself, I called my groups in class by their real names: "Ahead of Target," "On Target," "A Little Behind Target," and "Completely Clueless." The difference was the students in my class could self-select a group, and they could move up or down any day their status changed. This also left me free to devote special attention to those who were completely clueless, while independent readers could forge ahead. My group back in second grade was the top group, but even they were going so slowly that I thought I would go nuts. I read the whole book even as the teacher was telling us not to read ahead. Then I sat fiddling with the hem of my skirt or adjusting the book, my braids, or anything until it became unbearable. Once, struck with the abject absurdity of it all, I looked up and the ceiling and started to giggle uncontrollably. My teacher was not amused. She raised her voice at me, accusing me of making fun of the other readers. I remember trying to sputter an explanation, telling her I had just seen a spider on the ceiling, and it was making me laugh.

I did feel guilty. I certainly hadn't meant to make the other kids feel bad. Far from it. In fact I can still work up tears thinking about little Zobie Damron in that class. She fit in even less than I did. One day Zobie, in her plaid red full-skirted dress, came up behind me in the lunch line. Clutched in her fist was a little wadded-up handkerchief with coins tied in it. She offered to buy my friendship. Pause for sadness. This was the same little Zobie Damron who was angry with our horrible teacher, and when picked up kicking and yelling to be removed, grabbed the teacher's earrings right off of her ears and dashed them to the ground. She won my friendship that way for sure. I always championed the underdog, but I especially loved it when they championed themselves.

My teacher spelled helicopter wrong. She spelled it "*h-e-l-i-o-c-o-p-t-e-r.*" My dad was in aircraft, and I knew darn well it wasn't spelled with that extra *o*! I made the mistake of snapping and telling her. Whoops. "It's not *hee*liocopter, it's *helli*copter!" She was mad. Not sure what the punishment was, I think I only had to stand in the hall and think about what I had done, but when you're a little kid, an adult's disapproval is enough. I guess I didn't learn my lesson, though, even though I'm sure my mom would have cautioned me about correcting my teacher. How can you stand it when in second grade you have to tell your teacher, "It's not *p-o-s-s-u-m*; it's apostrophe *p-o-s-s-u-m*. It's got an apostrophe in front because the word is 'opossum'!" Well, how can you put up with a whippersnapper like Hannah Lynn? You don't—you send her to the principal's office. The shame. Mrs. Storment cemented my desire to become a teacher. I resolved to teach gifted children, so they would never have to suffer the boredom second grade had brought me. Wait—that means bad teaching can be just as inspiring as good! Maybe I should stop here?

When I can't sleep due to anxiety, I often go back through my memories of all the grades, as it seems to take me to a place in my brain that changes its frequency and lulls me to sleep. By third grade I often doze off, because it was uneventful. Mrs. Martin, I remember you, but mostly just your heart-shaped face and your full-skirted silky dresses. I wonder if anyone remembers only snippets of me like that – like how tall I was and how my colorful clothes earned me the name of "Skittles." Fourth grade, Mrs. Lawson, how sweet, patient, kind, and intelligent you were! You had a student teacher whom we found inspirational – she was a science-minded gal with very short blonde hair and tight skirts. She had worked for NASA! And brought wonderful scale models of the first ICBM's (Intercontinental Ballistic *Missiles*)! We received an education in science and women's liberation that year. But fifth grade came along to spoil everything again. Mrs. Helser didn't like me. I'm afraid I may have challenged her spelling a few times. Why hadn't I learned my lesson? This was not going to turn out well. She had her little pets who always got to erase the boards and be the leaders of groups; one was the blonde darling of the classroom, the other was her minion. I didn't stand a chance.

One day I stayed in at lunch and asked her, "Why don't you like me?"

She answered!

I couldn't believe she was actually giving me a laundry list. I told my mom, and she initiated a meeting with us and the principal. Mrs. Helser admitted that telling me she didn't like me had been wrong and was admittedly a bit kinder after that. I silently vowed not to say anything about her mistakes, even though it galled me to hold it in. By fifth grade I hated school. But sixth was another matter altogether.

Sixth grade brought a new-found dynamic to my life. I was a tomboy, tough as nails, and had earned the nickname Guts with my black windbreaker (boy) friends from my neighborhood. They went to my school, and I had a lot invested in impressing them. I really wanted to grow up fast. I had been reading Photoplay magazine for years, and thought I knew everything about Hollywood and modeling. I never read age-appropriate magazines (gag). So when sixth grade brought Mr. Mott, my first male teacher, I felt delighted and appreciated. He showed me a respect I hadn't felt before. Because he treated me like an adult —the way my beloved older brother treated me—I admired him. He was respected by all the kids in sixth grade because he was huge, spoke quietly and intelligently, and had interviewed for the CIA! We thought he was spy material and couldn't imagine why he chose teaching.

I had a huge beef with two of the girls in the class. Chris LeChrone (same blonde pet of all the teachers since her dad was District Attorney—big deal) was a really snotty girl. It didn't get to me when she didn't pick me for a team at recess, even though I could outperform most girls in baseball. What got to me was her cruelty towards others. We had a new girl in the class from Kentucky, Sharon Pendleton. She was obviously "different"—she committed the crime of having a little Southern accent and wearing the same plaid cotton dress more than once a week. Day after day she was left out of the games and stood alone with a sad little look on her face. Damn it, I just couldn't take it anymore. Chris was lingering with her minion, a little late to recess, as was I. She started in making fun of Sharon one more time, and I just snapped. I hauled off and slapped her across her face as hard as I could. I knew I would get in trouble for that. Apparently though, Chris finally got it that she had had it coming, because I never heard another word about it. Although I do not recommend violence as a solution to anything, that smack was deeply satisfying. Later in the year I began to wear lip gloss. The girls tried to get me in trouble for it. Mr. Mott said, "I think it looks nice." I don't know if he had any idea what an impact that simple declaration of support had on my self-esteem and strength to face the Chris LeChrones of the world.

My grounding in peace advocacy and civil rights began very early. The intellectual discussions around the table in our kitchen ranged from politics to religion to nuclear physics to psychology. If you wanted attention in our family, you'd say something informed. College was expected, we wouldn't have dreamed of not going.

President Kennedy died that year. We sixth graders were escorted across the parking lot to a portable building with a television set where we watched in awe. We sensed that we were considered the only class mature enough to see it. My parents were deeply opposed to U.S. involvement in Viet Nam and had already begun to teach us children about it. They had concerns about Kennedy's role in The Bay of Pigs. But they grieved him because of his humanity and his role in civil rights.

Mom made me translate Latin to her for a half hour every night. Both my older brother and sister took Latin from my mom, but I had to go to a different high school. She and I would sit companionably on the love seat in the family room with the fireplace and read together. She said that once I learned to read Julius Caesar in the original, I would understand why I was learning Latin, and she was right. *Vini, vidi, vici*! Julius Caesar was not only a brilliant (albeit evil) strategist, he was also a descriptive and entertaining writer. I learned how important Latin was to the furtherance of our educations. SAT vocabulary knowledge goes through the roof with all the Latin root words.

My brother John took salutatorian honors instead of valedictorian because of a cheating teacher who gave her own son an unearned better grade, thereby securing his miniscule grade point lead. I have absolute confidence that this story is true because of the integrity of my mother and brother. I was so crazy about my big brother. When he left home to go to Cal Tech, I was bereft, but I wore that blue Cal-Tech sweatshirt he sent me with a glowing pride. I was only eleven. His salutatorian speech was about planned obsolescence. In light of what we now know about landfills, plastics, and toxic e-waste, it was an amazing, forward-thinking speech. The intellectual level of the speech was so far in advance of today's typical high school valedictory speech, I have to laugh.

Seventh grade brought middle school, which we called junior high school, and where we had several teachers instead of one. I was banned from neighborhood sports by this time, because my beloved football friends had discovered I was a girl—I mean they knew I was a girl, but when I brought my arm back to throw a pass wearing a white blouse, Ralphie Thomas yelled out, "*Simpson,* you're wearin' a *bra!*" I hadn't needed one, but my precociousness had led me to want to wear one anyway. So I gave up on football. I feel like crying just thinking about it now. Football had been so thrilling. Nothing like catching that pass in the end zone. School physical education was a joke, with our little one-piece blue snap-up gym suits and our embarrassing showers.

I liked French, but I had studied privately with one of my dad's friends from France since fifth grade, so I was unavoidably annoyed with the teacher, who spoke with a Kentucky accent. I felt guilty for my prejudice, though, because she was nice. But all in all I felt well adjusted, learning Shakespeare, performing as Romeo in the balcony scene. I had cohorts, one of whom I vied with for the top or next to the top grade in every class. I took top in English, French, and social studies; he aced me out in math and science. It was really fun having rivalry and friends. But life is often capricious. Things were going so well, they had to change.

During the summer between seventh and eighth grade, my dad had to change jobs and we had to move two hours away to Indianapolis. Dad and I went for a couple of weeks ahead of my mom and sister to get the duplex ready (cleaning the floors, etc.) because he had to start his new job, and Mom was still teaching summer school in Vandalia. Our new neighborhood was an area with lots of trees, and a couple of families across the street had kids our ages. I managed to make friends and enjoy the summer even when my sister arrived to garner all the attention of some of the friends. But…I really missed all my friends from Vandalia.

One day I got the call that changed my life, just as most lives are changed the first time someone their own age, whom they know and love dies. My best friends in Vandalia were John and Linda Nohacs. The countless hours of playing baseball, football, war, and foursquare, running the streets most of the nights until way after dark every summer, we all shared so companionably. John Nohacs had been my defender when I was punched by Mike Johnston next door. He held Mike's arms behind his back in a gesture of fairness. I always stood my ground but having someone see justice in a similar light and demonstrate honor at the age of eleven really impressed me. I was always trying to be tough, taking all the mean shots boys could throw at me, to earn my right to run around in black nylon windbreakers and play pranks and jump fences and in general hang out with the guys. They were so much more adventurous than the girls, who wanted to stay in and play board games and dolls – which I also loved! But not like football.

My friend, the daughter of close friends of my parents, was the one who called. John Nohacs and his father had been up early on his paper route. A newspaper truck ran a red light into the intersection. Though John's father survived, John was killed. I couldn't believe I was two hours away and couldn't be with Linda, his beloved sister. I ached so badly it felt I would never recover. Everyone we knew was touched with the profound sadness of his loss. I began my writing at that juncture. Facing one's own mortality for the first time has a profound effect. The poem I wrote then wasn't very good, but it felt good to write it.

Losing a friend is like picking a fresh rose and placing it on the table.

You look again, and it has wilted.

You lock your grief in a room in your mind

Until a man called Conscious Thought

Ambles into the smothering darkness

He struggles to free himself from the oppression

But can never, never leave that room for good.

Eighth grade began, and life went on. I liked my school and began to make more friends—but then my parents found a house to buy, and we moved again. Eighth and ninth grade at Creston Junior High School for the Profoundly Upper Middle-Class was a nightmare for me. I was ostracized, hit repeatedly and spat on by boys who just didn't like me, insulted outright by rude girls for saying things like, "J.C. Penney is a nice store to buy clothes," or, "I don't think sex before marriage is necessarily evil." Funny, the girls who ganged up on me for saying that were the ones who had sex early, and I was the one who didn't. Educationally it was good—my English teacher asked the French teacher who should tutor her sons—and she recommended me. It was an honor. They came to my house for the sessions, and after the first lesson, I was asked not to frighten them anymore, I had shown them my bedroom with Beatles posters and hippie posters all over the walls and flower-child decorations everywhere. I didn't do that again and continued to teach them *français.*

My family was also ostracized by the community. I lost babysitting jobs because we had a big gold peace sign in the eaves of our house for Christmas decoration. A local preacher actually preached a sermon about my brother, because he came home from a summer working at our friend's ranch wearing a beard (how evil of him). I lost another babysitting job after that. The whole bullying thing at school got out of hand. When my mother got sick of it, she went to the principal and told him to get the parents in there. She warned that if her daughter ever came home with bruises again, there would be serious consequences. I never knew she had done this until much later. I just knew things began to improve a bit at least in terms of physical violence.

One boy had been hitting me and insulting me frequently, but for some reason I thought he was different. I teased him back. Years later when I was in California, he went to visit my parents and confessed he was sorry for how he had treated me and said he had always secretly admired me. I later heard he had taken too much LSD and ended up homeless living in a Kmart parking lot.

But my teachers' reactions are interesting to reflect upon. Once when I arrived in science class, one of the boys had spit in my chair. The hocker was huge and slimy. I stood in the aisle until the teacher had to ask me to sit down, at which point I went to the front of the room and told him, "I can't: they spit in my chair." That teacher lectured those kids for the rest of the period and even into the passing period. I knew I was gonna get it even more after that. These kids made a habit of hiding behind the stairwell and popping out to hit me as hard as they could in the tender part of the arm where the triceps and biceps join. But it was worth the risk of making it worse to see that *one* adult felt the injustice of their mistreatment and was angry on my behalf. A quite different experience occurred with my English teacher. He witnessed those boys taunting me mercilessly day after day, but when I finally used an expression I had never heard anyone use at school before—"*Fuck you!*"—I shall never forget that teacher's response. "Why, Hannah Lynn Simpson! I am so disappointed in you!" Wow. I was daily so disappointed in his knowing less grammar than I – *so what*. He made me sick.

I never forgot that lesson – and remember to tell my students every year that they must never respect *any*one who does not respect them. They must simply *behave* as though they do, to raise the standard of excellence, and never stoop to their level. Then—as my mother did—quietly seek redress! As a teacher, I was there to help students report when they complained about teachers who looked at their breasts or placed girls in the front of the room and "favored" the ones who showed cleavage. I was there to help report when a creep of a substitute teacher asked one of my girls to come to his house. I would go to the wall for any student who was made to feel uncomfortable or was asked to do something inappropriate. In fact, I delivered a ream of valid and serious complaint letters from students, but that is a story in itself, best left for Part III.

In my ninth-grade year, the strong feelings I experienced of rejection were overwhelming. I had cut my precious hair, which I had never cut since I was three years old, to try to fit in. I got contact lenses and I looked much more sophisticated. My parents spent a lot of money they could barely afford trying to make me happy, so that I could dress like the upper middle-class girls at my school. One *had* to wear tie Weejuns shoes in the dark reddish color known as cordovan, a Roderick St. John cordovan belt, and A-line or pleated wool skirts with matching sweaters. When one wore a cotton blouse, it had to have a pleat in the back with a little loop at the top of the pleat called a fruit loop, after the name of the cereal. The knee socks had to match the sweater.

We wore tights in the winter in Indiana, where it snowed. Girls were not allowed to wear pants even on the coldest of days. We had inside hallways, with lockers lining the walls. Our schools were pristine and sterile. I tried so very hard to make friends and fit in, but it never worked very successfully. Some girls would invite me to slumber parties, and I would host them at my house as well, but often there girls would be there who found me beneath them, and the resultant teasing was cruel. Once I wore a beautiful green rayon leopard-print jumpsuit with very stylish and flattering flared legs to a slumber party at the house of a cheerleader—one who wasn't stuck up and who treated me with respect.

But one other extremely popular and vacuous blonde cheerleader was there. She took one look at me and, snickering, said "You look like a piece of snot!"

The other girls fell into laughter as well; no one defended me. As we were falling asleep, the girls were discussing boyfriends. They talked about what they would get their boyfriends for Christmas. I didn't have a prayer of having a boyfriend, but I simply expressed what my mother had taught me, that you were not supposed to give personal items like cologne or clothing to the opposite sex, since that was considered too intimate. The other girls laughed themselves silly as I cried myself to sleep, the outsider.

Five foot ten by the eighth grade, with no figure to speak of, I was jeered at and laughed at. "Carpenter's Dream, flat as a board." "Stand sideways and swallow a pea and you'll look like you're pregnant." "Stand sideways and stick out your tongue, and you'll look like a zipper." Or just, "Ya big freak." I liked walking down the hall next to Gloria Curtley. Her mom was a lady wrestler, and Gloria was six foot three. I figured she made me look short. But even Gloria seemed to have more friends than I, and I spent most of my time on weekends and vacations from school at home reading. Reading was always my world. I had read *Jane Eyre* once a year for eight years, starting in fourth grade. Finding friends, especially a boyfriend, seemed hopeless. I went to dances at the local Y and loved to dance so much. Only once did a boy from our school take pity on me and ask me to dance for half a fast dance. I danced anyway. Sometimes I would hear kids complimenting my dancing, but they would never say it to my face.

When I was fourteen, my sister took me to her college to visit during a break. She attended freshman year at a very liberal arts school: Antioch College in Ohio, a highly-ranked school known for beatniks and then hippies. When I arrived, I had just had my hair cut for the very last time. I knew I would never have it cut again since I hated myself for doing it in the first place. My Dad had been a hairdresser in Hollywood in the 1930's. He was good at cutting hair, so I trusted him to cut it short one time, just to see what it was like. Indeed it was a good cut, and I had good, quality, stylish clothes, so I was happy to go visit my sister's college and find out what was up. This was a pivotal experience in my life. When I arrived at the dorms, I saw students hanging out of upstairs windows yelling down happily. Everyone seemed gleeful. I learned they were taking THC, the chemical in marijuana that makes you high. They showed me some of the little white tablets. I was afraid to take one, and I wasn't interested because so much else was new and fascinating.

My sister showed me to her dorm room and introduced me to college-age boys. She told me she had asked Mom for the pill since she planned to "do it" with a guy she had a crush on. I was completely, completely shocked. I cried and told her she was going to ruin her life... and what about her wedding night? (At this age, I hadn't yet had much conversation about sex.) Wouldn't her husband know she wasn't a virgin? The trip wasn't as fun for me after that. But she took me to a dance on campus called "Div Dance," the dance celebrating the end of the division (which was what Antioch called quarters). It was there that I was asked to dance my first legitimate dance, all the way through the dance. I was so excited my head nearly popped off. I was accepted by a male for a very rare moment in my life. And he was *Black!* I had never even *met* a Black person before! I knew my dad would have killed me if he found out. Once my aunt had seen my sister sitting on a bus stop bench with a Black man, and immediately called Dad: "I saw Mary Alice with a nigger!" My dad hit the roof, so I knew the consequences.

I know I looked a lot older than my years because of my height. I happily danced a couple of dances when the young man asked me something about school. I said I had just graduated. He asked me from where, and I said, "Creston Junior High School." When he heard I was so young, he simply took hold of my hand and led me back to my sister. Placing my hand in hers, he said, "Take good care of her," and bowed out ever-so-politely. I returned to my little world feeling the possibility existed that I would not remain lonely forever, though it was going to seem like it for quite some time to come.

When I got back home, I expressed my fears to Mom, still shocked that she had allowed my sister to go on birth control pills. My mom calmly told me that she did not consider pre-marital sex to be immoral, but that to bring a baby into this world whose parents were unprepared for parenting would be the greatest sin imaginable, and she would kill us if we did something that stupid. She explained about abortions, and that her brother had taken his daughter, my beautiful cousin, to Mexico for an abortion when she was around eighteen. I could not understand why it was not legal in the United States. She was so rational. I could barely wrap my head around her words, but they in fact did make sense, and I learned that day that women had choices, and they weren't as dire as they had been for my mom's generation. She told me that when I was ready, I was to be sure to ask her for the pill.

That experience also led me to want to expand my horizons. The First Lady, Ladybird Johnson, had spearheaded the Head Start Program initiated by JFK for preschool children whose parents could not afford private preschool. I volunteered at sixteen to go to the inner city of Indianapolis, a predominantly Black neighborhood that had many a lesson in store for this girl. I loved working there! I was looked at with some suspicion by the Black women teachers, but they kindly showed me the ropes. I quickly learned how to prepare snacks from the government cheese, which came in big blocks, the government peanut butter, which came in huge tin cans, and the government saltine crackers. I loved reading to the children, whose accents delighted me. I could tell what the kids were saying at the preschool, and I found the cadence and candor so enchanting. I still remember one little boy in particular, Reginald Poole, a charming four-year-old who loved my reading before naps. I read a story from an Uncle Wiggly book, where Uncle Wiggly always went to the barber shop. In those days, barber shops had red and white peppermint-striped barber poles. As I read this to him, Reginald piped up, "That ain't no barba pole. Y'all oughta *know* that ain't no barba pole." As I put Reginald down for his nap, he reached up and licked my nose. I think it was his way of satisfying his curiosity about my white skin, just as many white people who have never touched Black hair are fascinated, including me.

Ignorance of African-American experience was everywhere in the neighborhoods where I had lived. When I was very young in Vandalia, Ohio, I had seen a row of small white shacks lining the main highway through town. They were maybe 150 yards from my back yard, across a field. The other kids told me never to go over there because "colored people live there!"

I said, "There's no such thing as colored *people!*" I thought they meant pink and purple!

I went home and told my mom and she said, "They are talking about Negroes. Doctor King has asked us to call them Negroes."

I never gave it that much thought since it was apparently so taboo to go anywhere near those shacks. Those children lived within easy walking distance from us, but they never went to our schools, and I never saw them. Later I learned that they were migrant workers' children and lived there only seasonally. The only Black people I had ever seen in Ohio were downtown Dayton, men out sweeping the sidewalks, women at Woolworth's counter serving food.

My dad's sister once said of her suburban neighborhood in Dayton, "Those niggers are coming out like flies."

But at my home, my mother would sit in front of the TV watching Dr. King and explaining the plight of Black people in the world with love, compassion, and acceptance in her voice. She had been taught as a child by the Mormons that Black people were marked with the mark of Cain and destined to serve the white man even in heaven. The first Black people she ever saw were in Salt Lake City, where she, at eighteen, went to see the Harlem Globe Trotters. She took one look at them and said, "You think these people are inferior? You have *got* to be kidding." Mom left the church for their prejudiced views. We kids were brought up with no experiences of Black people, but certainly a wealth of things to read and to watch as the Civil Rights Movement unfolded before our eyes on television. We clutched hands in horror and cried together as we saw the German shepherd police dogs and the fire hoses turned on peaceful demonstrators.

I always thought my dad would one day see the light, as my mom explained that during his days as a hairdresser in Hollywood, dad's best friend had been Eddie Anderson, who played a very well-known part of Rochester on the weekly Jack Benny TV show. He was one of the few Black people ever seen on television. Of course, he played a servant. But Dad had that strange lack of ability to extrapolate and to see that if this guy were a great guy and a true friend, so could other Black people be much the same. He was raised racist and cantankerous, and never used his rational brain on what was a topic of argument in our family for many years. I was learning the lessons of the inner city and Black people from the teachers at the Head Start Program. I was learning the lessons of the poor. Once I asked why people in the neighborhood didn't mow their lawns. The teacher I worked with looked at me with hand on hip and said, "And where you gonna get the money for a lawn mower?"

These experiences motivated, shaped, and informed me. I read about Frederick Douglass in *Life Magazine*, and my mind and heart expanded with such respect and admiration. I began to rebel even more intellectually, extending my readings to the Socialist Workers' newspaper called *The Militant*. I got a subscription. I began to respect the Black Panther Party and wore black arm bands in support of their movement. Outside of the Head Start program, I didn't know any Black people, not really, and there were none in my school, so I was again ostracized, called "Nigger Lover," threatened, and punched. I identified with the peace movement and began to wear hippie clothing. There were few who cared about such things at my high school my junior year, so it was a lonely path.

I felt trapped in the Midwest. I began to experience the feeling of numbness, so much so that I later understood how young people could self-mutilate, in an attempt to exchange pain so deep it numbed psychologically, so that feeling physical pain was one of the only ways to know one was truly still alive. I remember thinking, I've got to get out of here or I am going to stab myself in the thigh. My parents thankfully recognized that I was getting a bit desperate and sent me to spend the summer with my brother in Los Angeles. I can never express how much that changed my whole perspective on who I was and what the future might hold. Instead of being made fun of, hit, spit on, and degraded, I was appreciated, respected, allowed to express myself, and spent some quality time alone at the beach with Led Zeppelin on the headphones and lots of great adventures.

My brother John worked at UCLA, and I got to hang out there sometimes, too. I watched NASA's moon landing in the office of one of his colleagues in the computer building. I was treated to movies at the theater on Figueroa where John introduced me to foreign films of Truffaut and Bergman and Fellini. But the coolest thing of all was seeing John at work at the Free Clinic in Hollywood, where hippies and drug addicts came for counseling. He let me hang out and "rap" with the street people, in the area where our dad used to be "Monsieur Bernard" of Hollywood, on Sunset and Vine. The neighborhood, of course, had changed, and yet there was a sense of connectedness that I think both John and I felt to that particular spot.

John gave of himself freely not because he had to, but because he was born with a gift of listening well and genuinely caring about the health of his patients. He always gave people the feeling that he was strong enough to hold on to their problems and shoulder them for a while, while they took a rest and tried to heal. His example was a great boon to me in my future career as teacher. We lost John to ALS recently, and I can't stop thinking about how he responded as he read the first part of this book. When he said it *would* get published, it elevated my self-esteem and encouraged me to persevere. I can't help wishing he were still here to talk it over. I feel like I still have so much to learn from him.

Returning to senior year was a lot easier after that. I saw the light at the end of the tunnel and knew that California would be my college destination. Because I carried myself with much more confidence, suddenly the other students who felt drawn to hippie consciousness were surrounding me, asking my advice, following my style, and I had friends. One cheerleader who had been part of the in crowd admitted senior year that she thought I was smart and had always admired me, even though her clique had shunned me since junior high. Being seventeen has that effect on young people. I have since witnessed seniors make remarkable changes as they all eventually begin to think about the world beyond high school that awaits. I kept my grades up, did well on my SAT's, but didn't really have the motivation to go straight to university. We were busy going to be-ins and love-ins at the park, where redneck students from my high school threatened to come after us with baseball bats and tire irons. We were learning about the war in Vietnam, protesting, working for the true peace candidate, Senator McCarthy, and were at McCarthy campaign headquarters when Robert Kennedy was assassinated. I remember we swarmed out into the street to go to comfort the young people only a block or so away who had been working at the Kennedy campaign headquarters. We were unaware of the overwhelming reaction that was to occur, we only knew how very sad and disappointed those other kids our age must have been, and we wanted to be with them. I am sure most of them then chose McCarthy when it came time to vote.

Before the shooting of white students at Kent State in Ohio, one girl had visited Indianapolis and hung out with our hippie group. A few days later her picture was the iconic image of the girl on the cover of *Newsweek Magazine*, arms to the sky, kneeling over the dead body of an innocent kid, shot by those very National Guardsmen who were supposed to "guard" the citizenry.

"Tin soldiers and Nixon's comin'/ We're finally on our own/ This summer I hear the drummin'/ Four dead in Ohio. / Gotta get down to it/ Soldiers are gunnin' us down/ Shoulda been done long ago/ What if you knew her and/ Found her dead on the ground? / How could you run when you know?" [v]

The night of high school graduation, I moved in with some friends in downtown Indianapolis, the Black neighborhood where I had taught preschool. The plan was to hang out there until I moved to California in fall. But there was nothing about living poor that was edifying. When I was awakened by shots in the night to discover next door neighbors were shooting at rats in the back yard with a .45, it was painfully obvious that I knew nothing about living in the ghetto. I was warned by my friends to take both dogs with me when I walked to the corner market. I couldn't understand why until they told me that the local Black folks seemed to have been picking targets for shootings and attacks, retaliating for the way they had been treated by cops for so long. One week it was open season on cops, and several had been shot or shot at from rooftops. The week before I got there, explained my hosts, it had been white women that were targeted, and one had been killed, her head smashed into the pavement. So I took the German shepherds with me, and began to plan my escape back to suburbia, which was looking pretty good; its boring sameness suddenly a welcome relief.

"Life in the hood/ Is all good for nobody." [vi]

I said goodbye to my friends from the rock band out of Chicago called Coven, whose fake brand of Satanism was a joke for all of us, and whose one hit, "One Tin Soldier," was the theme song for a popular martial arts movie called *Billy Jack*. Their friends, who owned a magic shop downtown, had hosted my stay. I often wonder what prompted my white friends to stay on in the Black ghetto, displaced white persons with stories of their own. Tom and Missy had been kind to me, but it was time to move on.

In June 1970—the month I turned eighteen—my parents took me to Europe for a whirlwind tour of London, Paris, Madrid, and Rome. Mom got a discount for taking some of her Latin students, enough to pay for me and my father. It was glorious, unforgettable. Mom had studied the classics in Rome for eight weeks one summer, and was the best tour guide, as she loved the Roman ruins like no other and happily explained their history and beauty. Mom and I did things the others were too lazy to do, and I will forever treasure that last early morning jaunt on the underground to the British Museum, where the Elgin marble took my breath away. The highlight of The Winged Victory of Samothrace at the Louvre, Michelangelo's Pieta at Saint Peter's Cathedral, El Greco paintings at Del Prado Museum, and watching flamenco dancers while drinking sangria in the grotto nightclub in Spain—I treasure those memories. I won't forget the people: the warm affectionate Italians, the proper British, fun French townspeople, and poetic Spaniards. My brother met us in Southern France and took me for the ride of a lifetime on his motorcycle.

I learned, and later, the travel informed my teaching. Communication through a shared willingness to negotiate for meaning was the most important.

"Stony limits cannot hold love out/ And what love can do, that dares love attempt..." [vii]

I loved it all. We viewed Europeans with open minds, and unlike so many of the "Ugly Americans" who used Europe like their personal Disneyland, we were able to mix with the folks of each area on a much more personal level—because they never suspected we were Americans. Everywhere we went we saw loud Americans littering and treating Europeans like their personal servants. White older American ladies all had short, permed hair, often dyed a bluish shade. Our mom had always worn a natural braid wrapped around her head. Our shoes were different because we dressed for walking. Because many of these countries were dependent upon tourism, they put up with a lot from the ugly Americans, but because of our appearance and demeanor, we were taken for British. Apparently British on holiday weren't quite as despised. We were also not anxious to be associated with the Vietnam War America was perpetrating at the time.

Europeans, especially in small towns, were lovely to get to know. Certainly knowing a bit of the languages helped, but it was fun to use sign language or whatever we needed to get where we were going. Later, I appreciated this experience when teaching English to immigrant students. I remembered what it felt like to try so hard to make myself understood. When I studied Vietnamese for six weeks in a night course for educators, I really got a taste of what it was like for newcomers. It took me that long to learn just a few phrases! The experience taught me that it would be extremely difficult to do what we asked our students to do in the few short years we give high school students—learn another language and culture well enough to graduate with their peers in all their subjects, which we taught in English.

When we returned from our trip, I prepared to move to California. Mother and I agreed that she and I would drive across the country to drop me off in Southern California. I said goodbye to my mom with a sense of freedom and carefree anticipation, and stayed at my brother's apartment in L.A. He was out of town at the time, but his friend, whose friendship I cherish to this day, graciously helped me go apartment hunting in Orange County, so that I could start school in fall of 1970. Now, 50 years later, that same friend has helped with the final edit of this very book.

Close Encounters of the Black Panther Party Kind

My first roommate, with whom I shared a room in a triplex where another student had her own room, was Kit Becker. Kit went to high school in the Midwest as well. We were to share an experience that I now consider one of the most fascinating of my life. A musician friend of mine invited me to a "convention" where he was going to play music, and he asked me to bring my roommate along to double date with his friend. We were all white.

It was the Los Angeles of 1970. We pulled into the area, parked, and began to walk toward the Los Angeles Convention Center. About four blocks from the center, I began to notice that the streets were filling with Black people, all heading in the same direction. Curiouser and curiouser. As we neared the entrance, I spotted guys in black berets with rifles – and cartridge belts across their chests. (!) Ohhhhh...You didn't tell me it was a *Black Panther Party* Convention! Then the friend proceeded to rebel against being searched in the lobby! I was thinking, *Wrong time, wrong place for a white guy to rebel. Geeze.* He was upset because they had been *asked* to play there. They explained that the keynote speaker had had several death threats. So we obviously had no choice but to consent to being searched. I looked back at Kit and her eyes were as big as saucers. Two out-of-place white girls with two strange uncommunicative white guys. We were ushered to the front row. I nervously took a glance behind me at the sea of faces, none of whom seemed the least bit interested in us, but I couldn't help but feel conspicuous and slouched in my seat until the lights went down and the speaker took the stage. It was pure fascination from that point on, as the speech was eloquent and riveting.

Later, as the four of us sat at a restaurant *not talking* about the convention, I thought to myself, *I never want to see these guys again.* To be so quiet that you do not communicate about such an experience... I was intrigued by the whole phenomenon, and yet there they were as though nothing had happened. Kit and I went home, stunned. I often wonder if she remembers it as vividly as I do. I witnessed a moment in history that would shape my philosophy and lend a new perspective to my already rebellious stance.

Hell, No! We Won't Go!

I had gone to several be-ins and love-ins in the parks of Indianapolis, where we mixed with other souls and shared flowers and mind expansion. Meeting some of my sister's interesting friends in the Los Angeles area helped me to actualize the protestor inside my soul. I marched in front of the federal court house in Los Angeles with peace posters and attended the trial in federal court of a draft-resistor friend of my sis. He was tried in front of a judge who was clearly senile and unfit for the bench. He said, "When I saw you the last time, I told you: 'He who represents himself has a fool for a client.'" There had been no last time. That was our friend's first appearance before that judge. This did not bode well for the outcome of the trial. He was sentenced to two years in federal prison. The young man was a noble soul whose non-violent resistance proved his willingness to sacrifice to avoid killing the Vietnamese, whom he considered no threat to us.

My sister and her soon-to-be husband met at Joan Baez' non-violent coordinating committee live-in seminar. I was inspired by them. The whole world seemed to be on the verge of an awakening—the dawning of the Age of Aquarius. "What if they gave a war and nobody came?' was my favorite poster. It seemed that change was gonna come.

The United Farm Workers Union

Cesar Chavez' s movement impressed me and touched my heart in a way that was to shape me further and help me to understand the many struggles of my students who were legacy children: Dreamers—children or grandchildren of the vast population of migrant workers found in California and throughout farming communities across the country. If we took a ride out into the desert in Southern California, we used to see lone souls coming from the border, walking, walking, walking. Once a friend and I stopped to pick up a young man, probably only fifteen or so. We gave him a gallon of water and a blanket and sandwiches. He had crossed near Indio and was walking to a destination at least a hundred and fifty miles away. The hope in his hand was a postcard, worn and crinkled from his pocket, saying there was work in Salinas.

All I have to do is to go on Facebook or watch news for a few minutes before I get extremely angry at what I am seeing from people who hate Mexicans. You aren't fooling anybody by saying you are only against illegal immigration or foreign ownership. You don't seem to care about the property held in the United States by Canadians or British. You don't care about those white immigrants whose accents are "charming," while you get pissed off when you have to be patient while giving an order to a fast-food worker whose accent or understanding of English is a little bit slower than you would like. You get your food. You get your food because undocumented workers are breaking their backs picking it for you. I taught hundreds of children of undocumented workers or those who had no papers themselves: any of them would be welcome at my table.

In the '70s I sometimes stayed with friends in the Los Angeles United Farm Workers Union house on Western Avenue. I learned that the huge homes there, run-down by the '70s, were once the neighborhood of the first upwardly-mobile class of African-Americans in the Los Angeles area, the first Black doctors, lawyers, and professionals. Of course there was de facto segregation, so the neighborhood had been all Black families. By the seventies, the Union had set up the house for its volunteers, who went out by day to picket Safeway markets and other stores who sold produce from farms whose owners would not allow the Union to organize. There were horrifying incidents of violence to workers who tried to get together and hold elections. The growers employed Teamster thugs to attack the Mexican and Filipino workers with weapons, including but not limited to tire irons, guns, and knives.

The cry of the protestors was, "There's blood on that lettuce!"

No matter how many times the produce managers washed those grapes, artichokes, lettuce, there would always be blood. The volunteers came from all over the country, stood together, signs held defiantly, yelling to shoppers, "Boycott!" As we joined hundreds of other Farm Workers Union volunteers across the nation, the nation joined us, and the first successful boycott of a major corporate interest was forced into capitulation. All they were asking for was the right to unionize for clean drinking water and bathrooms in the fields! Can you imagine being denied these *basic* human rights while working for the profit of those few who lived in the big houses? Sound like shadows of slavery? The fact that other unionized workers were the ones hired to terrorize immigrant workers stood as stark proof of the racist nature of the overlords and their overseers

Consuelo G. Hendrix

Our younger daughter is named Rainy Consuelo Demerson. The Consuelo comes from a friend who profoundly changed my way of looking at life. Born the daughter of Mexican parents in Tucson, Arizona, Connie was my supervisor when I went to work at Fairview State Hospital. The ward where we worked housed the "profoundly retarded." We no longer use those terms, thank heavens. These were individuals whose IQ would range sometimes as low as four to eight, although I never could imagine how one could measure IQ so low. One telling factor was that they could rarely learn to feed themselves from a spoon. Many were not toilet-trainable and required huge cloth adult diapers. Most were non-verbal. Connie was the psychiatric nurse in charge of the ward. I was designated one of the "hospital workers" who cleaned the wards and transported patients.

It had to be the dirtiest job on the planet. We were expected to clean the urine, feces, mucous, and vomit, which were always to be found on every surface, in all the crevices of all the furniture, on the toilets, in the beds; and sometimes we helped clean the patients themselves, although technically that was the domain of the Psychiatric Technicians. I made very close friends there, because to work there and not go crazy put one in a special club, a club of survivors who could either bond and get the job done in the most expedient and humane way possible, or give up. My new friends were the young Mexican women who worked there and taught me that no job is so low that one cannot find a way to take pride in doing it the best way possible. We worked so hard sometimes the tears would pop out and stream down my face when I wasn't even sad—I was just so tired that my tear glands could not hold the tears in my eyes any longer. But that ward was clean by the time the night shift arrived, by damn.

Night shift Techs could tell when I or my friends had been there because they could smell the bleach when they walked on the ward. Some of the lazier hospital workers never even bothered to clean out the mops at end of shift, leaving them to stink up the utility room. I won't name all the other nasty surprises left for others to clean. It was so difficult to get fired working in the state system, that even slackers went unpunished. We who decided that honest work was more to our liking than getting away with slacking, we loved our supervisor, Consuelo G. Hendrix. She taught us to respect that which was righteous, and to stand up against that which was not, by her fierce, take-no-prisoners attitude toward all her nemeses. And there were plenty.

The white men who ruled the wards were forced to accept her ways because she was brilliant, and her nursing skills and compassion were unassailable. They needed her, yet they never stopped trying to blindside her, derail her best intentions for improvements, stab her in the back, and then smile and say they wished her well. After treating her like the effluvia that we had to clean, they had the nerve to hold a going-away party for her. She took the chocolate cake they offered her and tipped it right into the boss man's face, icing and all. Her determination was so intense that I was drawn to her the moment I met her and began to seek her advice on a regular basis. She was there when I decided to break out of a five-year relationship with an abusive boyfriend. This is how it went down:

Me: "I wish I could move in with you."

Connie: "You'd hev the time of your life."

I did, and I did. I rented a room in her home, and often she would give me a ride to work on her motorcycle. Connie had four children by her first husband, and I learned from her family many interesting aspects of their Chicano way of life. I was living there when Connie quit her job at the State Hospital and was hired by Governor Jerry Brown's Agricultural Labor Relations Board. Her family members worked hard for the United Farm Workers, and Connie was anything but sympathetic to growers. She told me of the fields hidden away from the eyes of freeway drivers, where little children slept in the rain and mud on plastic garbage bags. Where human beings were intimidated and had no rights to organize.

But when the governor called, she told him, "Jerry, if you want me to be unbiased, then I will be unbiased."

Of course, her "lack of bias" was the reason the growers sent a hit man to try to kill her in her hotel room while she was in Indio working on arbitration. He assaulted her, held a knife to her throat.

But Connie said, "Henna, I just looked into his eyes; I looked into his soul; and he could not do it."

That same fierce look served her again in court when she went to Arizona to claim custody of her two nieces in the courts. She again described looking into the soul of the judge, so that judge had to see her determination to protect those girls from a life in the hands of the system. Connie rebelled so many times that she was taken to jail for resisting arrest, for refusing to pay for her dog's assaults on other dogs, and once for having to be dragged out of the window of her own car for refusing to exit the vehicle. She was ferrying a drunk ex-husband home after the bar he'd been drinking at called her to come and get him. His drunk head flopped into her lap, causing her to swerve a little on the freeway. She told the officer: "Can't you see that *he* is the one who's drunk?" As they dragged her kicking out of the car window, she managed to pull a little bit of one officer's ear off. She just wasn't having any of it. She used to carry pictures of her brothers and sisters in her wallet, but one picture was just a cartoon of a pig. She told me, "Oh. That's my brother Bucho. Hees a pig." Bucho was a policeman in Arizona.

Still, I think of Consuelo as the most gentle and loving woman, because she saved all her considerable grace for the people whom she truly respected and gave absolutely no respect to those who didn't. Her fearlessness helped me to see life in sharper focus than ever before. It was through her dauntless behavior that I became emboldened to effect many changes in my life, among them leaving that bad relationship, and consequently leaving my heart open for the one true love of my life.

Charles E. Demerson

When I met Charles, I was out dancing at an all-Black nightclub in Santa Ana called Alias Smith and Jones after a long swing shift at the hospital. We fell in love that first night on November 19th, and were married nine weeks later, January 28, 1977. Charles had told me all about his family of thirteen brothers and sisters the night we met. When he called to tell his deeply spiritual and loving mother about me, he said, simply, "She's Irish." I took a deep breath as he put me on the phone with her. I shall never forget the tone of her words, the words themselves, nor the warmth that came through all those miles of phone wire from Houston, Texas. "I told my son, 'I love whoever he love.'" If you could only know how much those words meant, and how simple it made our decision seem. Our hearts were full of the love of each other, and that was it.

I did not tell my parents because my father had already disowned me when he found out I was *dating* a Black man. I knew it was going to be hard on my mom to deal with my dad. On Thanksgiving when my parents came to California to be with us kids, I sort of kidnapped my mom and drove her down to San Diego area to meet Charles in his hotel room. I simply explained on the way there that there was someone I wanted her to meet. Charles and she had a wonderful conversation, while mellow R 'n' B music played on the stereo in the background. I remember the fancy shirt he wore; I remember his offering her anything she might want to drink. Afterward he summed up his first impression of her: "Your mother loves tradition. But she loves knowledge more than she loves tradition." This was such a perspicacious commentary after having met her for only a few short hours.

On the way back to my brother's house, I told Mom, "We most likely *will* be getting married."

She began to cry. "But what about the children?" She knew it wouldn't be a bed of roses.

I told her that studies I had read recently in *The Nation* magazine showed that mixed children were actually bringing both races together. If it was in *The Nation,* Mom was much more pre-disposed to acceptance. I told her that any children I had would be "different" anyway, and we would just deal with it the same way our parents had helped us. She calmed down a bit, but I still knew my dad would make her life quite challenging once he found out.

Charles never had to ask me to marry him. He just said one day, "By the way, when *are* we getting married?" Then a few weeks later he called from the Marine Corps base at Camp Pendleton where he was a sergeant, to say, "Can you get a blood test this week? I'd like to get married this Saturday." I was so excited. Only my brother and sister with her baby son and one friend from work came to the ceremony at the Orange County Courthouse. My brother was so nervous, he messed up the wedding photos. Only a few close friends joined the wedding party at the Chinese Restaurant afterward for a meal and good conversation. We took off in our VW van the next morning for a camping honeymoon on the beach in Baja, California. It was glorious. But my parents still did not know.

I called my mom one morning at four in the morning in April and told her. I told her she did not need to tell my dad unless she wanted to. I would leave it up to her. But he did find out. A first stroke had left his personality significantly altered, and apparently, he reacted by doing some rather heavy drinking and swearing and crying. He died of a second stroke before he ever met his son-in-law or granddaughters. I had always held out hope that he would have eventually come around. Just before he died, I sent him a letter in which I explained that I still loved him, and that marrying Charles was not done to hurt him.

The first thing I asked my mother the night she called to say that he was gone was "Did he get my letter?"

And she said that he had read it and had been smiling.

I hold on to that.

Learning to Teach

Connie, Mother, and of course Charles encouraged me to pursue my dreams of teaching. I wanted to become a Montessori teacher for three- and four-year-olds because they are just so cute and responsive. Charles told me after knowing me only one month, that whatever line of education or career path I chose, he would pay for it. I chose the Roston Montessori Teacher Training Program in Orange County. Mrs. Roston was Indian-born, and had been directly taught by Doctor Maria Montessori herself. When Mrs. Roston was a little three-year-old girl, Dr. Montessori had been exiled from her home in Italy to India during the Second World War. She actually lived with Mrs. Roston's family. This level of authenticity impressed me. I learned a tremendous amount from Montessori teacher training; in fact, I think it was one of the only trainings I ever needed to equip me for a career in education. Reading the works of Dr. Montessori alone would help anyone establish a much more useful approach than all of the other workshops, staff meetings, principal speeches, No Child Left Behind, Common Core, or standards trainings combined.

When I began my internship in the Roston schools, I taught four-year-olds to read. I worked and learned and loved it all. But as fate would have it, one day they asked me to substitute for the private Montessori high school class they had going at that campus. I remember walking in and seeing a haze and smelling a locker-room smell. The kids had been playing roller ball around the classroom, and the haze was steam their bodies had created as they caromed off of the walls! That was a challenge that took possession of me. I wanted to find a way to have them settle and learn something that day. Within a half hour, the students could be found in their desks, waving their hands excitedly, trying to learn, of all things, grammar! I couldn't have been happier and decided that very day that I was to become a high school teacher. My best friend once read something about me that said, "You love to create chaos. But you love to create chaos, so you can create order from that chaos." I think that statement, if anything, may best describe my teaching style.

Learning from world class linguists about second language acquisition was the only other training that came close to matching Montessori method training in its relevance and immediate applicability in the classroom. As for so-called "Methods" class at university, I felt like I should have been teaching it myself. I went to my advisor in secondary education once enrolled in that program at San José State University and asked that sage professor if I could somehow opt out of "Methods." She handed me a stack of textbooks ten high and said read these and report back to me with written summaries of their most salient features. When I did this, she put me on a fast track to skip "Methods" and head straight for creating lesson plans, plans that I used with variations until the end of my career. Every year I adapted the lessons because the classrooms filled with different children, and there were new challenges to adapt to and to tweak. Dr. Alice Scoffield told me that my lesson plans were lovely and intricate, but asked how would I propose to use them with one hundred and fifty individuals? My eyes were opened that day. It had never really hit me that the sheer number of students was going to make all that individualization a logistical nightmare. I struggled to individualize education throughout all my years of teaching. Diversify and individualize but reach them all and grade them all in some sort of fair and equitable fashion. Use authentic assessment but prepare the students for standardized testing. It reminds me of the lady who took anger management and assertiveness training at the same time. Her head exploded.

While Montessori teacher training, I was working as a Teaching Assistant with "profoundly retarded" students at the state hospital who unlearned every activity if you missed one day with their practice. Charles and I lived in Costa Mesa, California to be near my work and in the vicinity of the Marine Corps base at Camp Pendleton. He commuted early in the mornings.

Once I was taking him there in our VW camper van, driving along the coast as we looked at the beautiful and expansive morning vistas over the ocean, Charles said, "If we have a girl we'll name her Spirit, and if it's a boy, we'll name him Sky."

I was in love with those names instantly. I became pregnant and one day looked out at the sky and heard a voice say, "I am still out here, and Spirit is inside you." Indeed, although all the doctors predicted a boy, my baby was to be our girl Spirit.

When Charles was discharged from the Marine Corps we moved to Houston. Living near his mother and feeling her unconditional love surround me, I learned to love his family and appreciate the experiences that had molded his character. The neighborhood in which he had been raised was an all-Black neighborhood, the street one of the poorest in the city. But not *the* poorest. I saw buildings in Third Ward that looked as though they had been bombed out, buildings that looked like Lebanon or Dresden after the fire-bombing but overgrown with those rotten stinking ubiquitous plants that choke everything that is untended in the humid South. Then Charles told me people lived there, and my jaw dropped. This level of poverty was a disgrace in a nation as rich as ours, a state as rich as Texas.

Charles enrolled at the University of Houston and elicited my help with his reading and homework. He was really struggling. He was, of course, working and going to school at the same time, and the load was very difficult. I was working part time and heavily pregnant, but eager to help him.

The U of H campus was quite nice—urban, but well-tended. Literally right across the expressway was Texas Southern University, the HBCU (Historically Black University) that Charles had attended briefly before joining the Corps. It was completely run-down, and the grass was brown, untended, looking for all the world like the ugly stepsister to U of H. In fact, an ongoing Justice Department investigation proved that funding for U of H had been misappropriated, and that Texas Southern had been illegally underfunded for upkeep. It was demonstrated that the racial disparity was indeed intentional, and the funding was ordered to be evenly dispersed after that ruling. Charles decided to go to Texas Southern to see if it would help his grades. In fact, with the help of a brilliant instructor who understood just how "Black talk" was holding students back from achievement in English, along with courses heavily dependent on writing skills, Charles learned accelerated English standardization and returned to courses at U of H to earn A's in English.

A Black woman who knew just what Charles had gone through, that instructor taught him advanced vocabulary and usage. I learned from her example that one must not mince words, one must acknowledge that "Black talk," as culturally creative and interesting as it is, is not going to help Black students pass standard English tests. Ebonics was made up to explain Black talk, which is a truly fascinating socio-linguistic phenomenon. I almost changed my major to socio-linguistics, after a course in which I studied the history of West African language features and how they influence American Black talk to this day. It is a testament to how strongly a people can sustain a culture, even though it has been systematically and violently smashed by the ruling oppressors. But it is not the way to earn good grades in "the system."

As Maya Angelou made clear in her memoirs, learning Shakespeare and the so-called most eloquent of the English language authors made it possible for her to enter the world of whites and conquer their conventions, while maintaining her style choices when she chose to speak as her family spoke. Having a choice to use standard forms and switch to Black talk when you want to is like having the choice between standard English and Spanglish or the myriad other pidgins of English. The goal, as I heard described once in a very pointed article, is *to reach the broadest possible audience, because what you have to say is important.* That has been the standard by which I judge writing. Could this piece have been understood by a well-read fifth grader as well as appreciated by a college professor? Is it intellectually honest, and does it demonstrate reflection on something worth reflecting upon? To write like this requires standard conventions. Period. So teaching English means helping people like Charles bring their ideas forward to a broad audience. That brilliant mind of his can now reach everyone, and his memoirs will touch future generations. He still sometimes uses non-standard subject-verb agreement, and I still help him with it. But never will he be misunderstood, and that's because of his burning desire to learn and to educate. So Charles' professors taught me as well, as I sat at home pregnant and waiting to get back into my own courses, back onto my own professional path.

After Spirit was born, I went to work at an old folks' home as a dishwasher and server. Then I got a job at a high school for emotionally disturbed teens called Spring Branch Academy. That was certainly informative. Good grief. One student was there because he had held a knife to the principal's throat at his former school. I actually found him quite easy to get along with. One day he brought a bullwhip to class. Yes, a long, braided bullwhip, about six or seven feet long, in fact. He began to brandish the whip as other students moved toward the outer walls of the classroom. Hmmmm, what to do, what to do? Remain calm, remain calm, remain calm, remain calm.

Said I in a calming voice, "Oh, that is some beautiful braid work on that leather. May I see that?" He brought it to my desk and let me see it. I ran my fingers along the braiding, and then quick as a flash, locked it into my bottom desk drawer. I told him he would have to wait until later to play with it. Sheeeesh. The next incident with this particular student was when we teachers were on our way to an outside break. Another student had had a grand mal seizure and was resting on the mats on the floor inside a dimly lit classroom. As we passed by outside, we looked into the classroom to see that same miscreant trying to light the sleeping boy on fire with a cigarette lighter! The rascal showed very little affect as he was escorted to the administration. As though lighting kids on fire was a completely normal part of the school day.

I had some wonderful successes teaching novels to those students. I remember sitting outside doing a read-around of *My Darling, My Hamburger.* It had just enough craziness in it to increase students' interest. That was a very pleasant experience, with small groups, sitting under the trees. There I first learned about autism, and specifically brilliant autistic folks. I had a young Black student who was absolutely phenomenal at, for example, taking the back off of a '70s type radio, examining the circuitry briefly, closing it up, and drawing the intricate circuitry from memory, down to the slightest detail. He drew marvelous city skylines and grid diagrams of whole cities from memory but could barely interact with us. He was genuinely a nice fellow. I thought of Socrates and his methods, and I was content.

We had a law in Texas that we could restrain students who were out of control by placing them in a vertical box, where they could sit and see out, but not hurt anyone. I never saw the box mis-used by our excellent and compassionate staff, but I could certainly see the potential for abuse. I was impressed by the staff, who were professional, caring, and actually the most fun staff I ever had the pleasure of working with. I think a lot of this was due to the working conditions. Our small groups with low pressure to pass any kind of tests were ideal for improvising appropriate and helpful curricula. We also had half days on Fridays and went to a local restaurant to a large table where around pitchers of beer, we discussed our students, our goals, our curriculum, and laughed our way out of the shock, isolation, and depression that often accompany more traditional, straightlaced methods of working with emotionally disturbed individuals. I mean, when you have just taken away a bullwhip from a boy with a history of assault, you really need that camaraderie.

Charles had been working the job that it formerly took three men to do: lifting extremely heavy sheets of metal and dipping them into chemical baths, outside in over 100-degree heat. Then going to school after his long hard day. He was "let go" because the white boss wanted to hire his own nephew. Our kung fu instructor, another Black gentleman, worked in the affirmative action office at that company. He told Charles he could get his job back if he wanted to take action. When Charles went to the parking lot, some white rednecks rolled up in a pickup with shotguns, and told him, "You can come back, but we know where your wife and baby are."

We moved back to California, but Charles never told me about that threat until years later. I asked him why he had never said anything, but as he was telling me, I already knew the answer: I didn't need that worry, trying to nurse a new baby and adjust to working at a job with mentally disturbed individuals.

We moved in with my mom near lovely Los Gatos, California. Charles began his search for work again, we both enrolled in school once more, and soon we had enough money to move to our own apartment in Campbell. Our second daughter, Rainy, was born during this time, and I worked at Santa Clara High School as a classroom aide, which informed my teaching yet again. Each step along the way made me a better person and left me with a more profound love of the young people I served.

One day we showed a film in the special education classroom about poverty and Fetal Alcohol Syndrome on Native American reservations. A student said, "My dad told me that only Black people have the right to sing the blues." He looked up at me with a question in his eyes and made me cry, saying, "I think Native Americans have the right to sing the blues, too."

It wasn't always rosy. The summer before that, I had taught at a summer school where white elementary school kids made me crazy with their unbelievably bad behavior. I was kicked in the shins while supervising the playground, and I was five months pregnant. Those kids were a mess. They were far more ungovernable than the so-called emotionally disturbed kids had been. Their sense of entitlement was terrifying and disheartening. I taught only summer school in white schools, and each time it was a lesson in what I did not want to be doing. At Santa Teresa High in southeast San José, I was treated to angry calls from parents whenever their precious angel had not received the grade the parent thought was appropriate. Parents routinely did their kids' homework for them. I was berated by students whose ideas of their own importance were not met with acquiescence by me. I did not enjoy the pouty faces and the derisive "Why do we have to study Mexican writers?" I was reported on to principals by white and Asian students for teaching so many ethnic authors. Perhaps one might think that working in an urban school of minority students is challenging. But I could never have been as happy in affluenza-infected schools.

And yes, our schools are still segregated. Because as long as there are de facto red lines around real estate communities and banks refuse loans based on race, some communities still get to say Not In My Back Yard to low-income housing, we will continue to see Black and Brown and immigrants in enclaves. Meanwhile, the established, usually white people of means, or the upwardly mobile, continue to move to the suburbs. The suburbs where a father might walk into a classroom and say, "Oh, the students don't have computers?" And magically, the next day, a truckload of new computers arrives, courtesy of Dad.

As the first Black superintendent of East Side Union High School District used to say, "You don't have to sit next to a white kid to get a good education. You have to sit next to a kid whose parents went to college." And I say, statistically, if you *really* want to succeed, your grandparents need to have gone to college. Although many are able to buck this, the data is quite clear that you will need that level of educational background and sophistication to reach the highest echelons of education in this society. Over and over I saw the pattern repeated. Expectations were low because the students never saw anyone in their family navigate the getting-in-to-college experience. They did not know how to fill in applications. They were afraid to break out of the shell. They were afraid to leave home and face discrimination that was surely waiting for them at the universities. And they were right to be concerned! But still many of my former students are posting graduation from university pictures as I write. Many overcome the obstacles, but make no mistake about it, SAT scores correlate *exactly* with household income levels. That should tell us something about disparity.

I left San José State University having achieved my bachelor's Degree in English with Honors and my secondary teaching credential while having two small daughters, having had six foster children, and having helped my husband get his degree while he worked two jobs. I left having a burning desire to teach English, to teach it to adolescents, and to be an aid to life. I got my first job straight after my credential came through, and just in time, as my husband's GI Bill payments stopped the month before my paychecks began.

Part III

The Adults in the Environment, and How They Can Get in the Way of Teaching

Academic Freedom

In California, once a teacher has tenure, that teacher is usually given a fair amount of academic freedom by virtue of policy. This by no means signifies that one can teach whatever the hell one wants without being pestered by administrators, some of whom approach their job with an eye toward the improvement of the instruction, and some with an arbitrary and capricious desire to micromanage and control the school. I learned from conversations with my mother just what to expect. She told the story of one principal who ended every faculty meeting with an admonition that teachers must lower the blinds on their classroom windows two-thirds of the way down. "I want to drive away from the school at the end of the day, look back, and see a row of neat blinds exactly the same!" This is not a joke; this is a true story of a control freak who cared very little about academia or the students and staff. He just wanted what he wanted, period. New teachers should take this story as a cautionary tale.

Sometimes with administrators—just as with students on your roll sheets— "You got who you got." Your principal may drive you nuts with nit-picky little restrictions, and your job will be to continue to toe the line if you can, and to find what you are willing to tolerate for the sake of peace in the realm. Because it seems many teachers who do not actually like to teach in the classrooms are the very ones who decide to get administrative credentials and "move up" for a bit more power and prestige. I myself am guilty of having a controlling streak, so I understand what happens when one feels the pull of wanting things to move along according to one's own perception of order. As English department chair for fifteen years, I can say that very little was more satisfying than when teachers worked together to help create lesson plans, and to share portfolio writing experiences. But I was sometimes dictatorial, and I did not like that about myself. I also felt as though I would not like anyone else organizing the department: sometimes I had the heady experience of thinking I knew what was best for us. And I had very little patience for teachers on a slow learning curve, or teachers who wished to show off, not show up, or try to dominate meetings. So when I sensed our administrators were experiencing the same crises in leadership, I would support them, as long as I felt that what they were asking teachers to do would benefit the school as a whole and the curriculum in particular, as well as address larger school issues (such as extra-curricular activities, school maintenance, school-wide discipline, etc.). But when administrators were heavily into top-down management, did not seek input from teachers, and generally disregarded me in particular, I got my hackles up, and became unpleasant. This did not always work in my favor.

In the beginning, like all new teachers, I was on "probation" for three years. This means you could be fired if the principal or associate principal decided they didn't like you or your performance. They could do so with impunity, without strong reasons. After the probationary period, when tenure was conferred, a teacher could begin to flex her muscles a bit. But even during my probationary period, I could see ways in which the administration and I were going to have problems.

Let me take you to my first interview at William C. Overfelt high school. It was attended by the principal and two of the English department chairs. They were all men. They asked me the questions that I expected, and after hearing my background, complete with my experiences in education, they seemed positive. I thought the interview was going pretty well. The principal asked me if I would be able to be an assistant coach in girls' volleyball and basketball. I said, "Yes, of course," and went home and asked my husband how many people were on a basketball team. I had no clue. But I had played volleyball in college and thought that it would probably be fun to help out. And I could at least help with calisthenics and warm-ups for girls in basketball, since I was very fit from martial arts and yoga and knew a lot about the physiology of exercise. So when I said "Yes," it was a spontaneous ploy to get the job. But I figured, "Fake it 'til you make it," and it worked. After I broke my ankle playing volleyball at the local community college and had to spend the first few games hobbling about in a walker, I begged off.

The workload as an English teacher was incredible those first years, and my department chair supported me when I decided, "enough is enough." I found out that most new teachers are asked if they are willing to take on a lot of extra tasks, like a trial by fire. We caution English teachers to *just say no,* let the P.E. department, who do not go home to stacks of papers to grade, do the coaching. But new teachers don't always listen because...probation. Later they learn the common-sense rule of the military: never volunteer for anything (unless you are personally passionate about it) because your rewards will be longer hours, little or no remuneration, and certainly little or no real appreciation. Some highly successful coaches who stay on the good side of administration are given an approximation of respect. Most go unheralded, and the extra pay amounts to far less than minimum wage for the hours put in.

So if you really, really love your sport or club, go for it. You will get the opportunity to interact with students outside of the classroom and get to know interesting aspects of their personalities and talents that come out in a sports or club experience. Just know you are a volunteer and try not to expect support or recognition. Although I worked for years as the Feed the World Club advisor, putting my heart and soul and time and money into hunger awareness, I was passed over for the "Humanitarian" award every year. The award was always given to cronies of the administrators, whether they had accomplished extra duty or contribution or not. I should not have been surprised. My mother had told me many similar stories, and I never saw the administration support her efforts. She was rewarded in small ways, as good teachers usually are. By small gestures that melt the heart. I remember her telling my siblings and me of a big farm boy, awkward and shy, who was learning poetry in her class. She hadn't expected to get through to him. At the end of the year he came in to her classroom and dropped something into her hand. It was a clunky necklace, and a poem. She wore that necklace as though it were diamonds and treasured that poem as a symbol. All a teacher needs to fuel a whole year of dedication is one small gesture from someone who truly cares. If we can hang on to those moments, approval from administration becomes peripheral and sometimes even unwanted!

At the end of that interview at Overfelt, the three men were congratulating each other on having found me. They were saying things to each other, as though I weren't there. "I'm happy with her; are you happy with her?" said the principal. "I'm happy with her," said one department chair. They were shaking each other's hands and weren't even looking at me as I slipped out of the room. It was as though I were an acquisition that credited them, rather than a new fellow educator.

I guess one could say the reviews were mixed on my performance in the English department. I was frequently late because of home problems, though only by a few minutes. I guess one could say I didn't care quite as much about the virtue of being on time as I did about the virtue of getting my own children to school with a peaceful send-off, which was not easily accomplished in those days. When I arrived late back to class once, after going the three blocks home for lunch, I was met at my classroom door by three male authority figures, all using their walkie-talkies to communicate. One was the principal himself, one an associate principal, and one a security liaison. I felt a bit intimidated, but mostly a bit embarrassed. But not *that* embarrassed, more like, defiant. I guess I felt that it was what I delivered once I got there that mattered. And lord knows we teachers put in enough overtime after school.

When I told my mother about my tardiness, I expected her to scold me and say something about my lack of professionalism. Instead she simply said, "Well, Dear, they're just going to have to get used to you." *That* is the way to support a teacher. Unconditional faith that dedication to the students and to the profession is not measured by the little regimented behaviors that micro-managers love, but instead by the competence of the teaching and the responsiveness to students' changing needs. Mom always said, "Great principals hire the best people, then leave them alone to do their jobs."

I just wanted to be left alone to do my job. Visits from the principal were extremely annoying. Many sit in the back and nit-pick on paper. Many don't know what they are looking at, and don't understand the lesson in its entirety or how it fits into the larger curriculum. Some supervisors from the university programs are like that, too. One supervisor came to observe a truly gifted new teacher and ended up making her cry. One supervisor of one of my student teachers who, against my continued advice, was hashing over a lesson she had taught before in two other forms.

The students were actually saying out loud, "This is so boring!"

The supervisor told the student teacher, "I am glad you are able to take a story that students often don't relate that well to and make it so it isn't boring." Where had he been? Had he lost his hearing? Was he so out of touch with the youth in the classrooms of modern schools that he couldn't see her lesson wasn't cutting it? I just thought to myself, time will tell. I don't need to intercede because either she will figure it out on her own, or she won't, and the students will make her life miserable, and she will decide teaching isn't for her after all.

One morning early in my tenure, I was on my way to my classroom in the morning, when I related to some colleagues my horror at having seen an article in the newspaper about the firebombing by police in Philadelphia of an *entire block* of homes where Black families lived. It was the enclave of a group of Black folks called the MOVE organization. Neighbors had complained that as the enclave had been restricted with little income coming in, they had sanitation problems and their neighborhood had begun to stink. The police response was to firebomb the whole block. A whole block of men, women and children were assassinated in an American city. One little boy, only eight years old, was found *shot in the back by a police bullet* while trying to escape. Appalled and sickened, I planned to talk about this with my students that day. Two men, both wrestling coaches and all-around jerks, told me "Well, we can't use our position as teachers to talk about stuff like that."

My response: "I *am* gonna talk about it, you can *bet that.*" I'm sure it got around that I wasn't taking any crap from these guys. Not a popular position. But we call out injustices wherever they are found. If not from responsible adults, where will our students hear these important truths?

The current anti-police brutality movement is taking up the cry, and it is certainly a teachable time in history to encourage open discussion of injustice. I would take up the challenge now to teach about the rise of fascism as we see in the political situation we currently face. There are ample literary examples, especially speeches, through which one can explore the importance of rhetoric and the difference between rhetoric and propaganda in an English or social science class. Teachers who have told me that they do not wish to teach about controversy are cowards. It does seem that we risk when we speak out, but when our opinions are not just opinion but demonstrable facts, we can stand firm, knowing that there may be consequences, yet in the long run, the rewards far outweigh the consequences.

High school students do not like to be talked down to, nor do they appreciate lies in their textbooks. When I call out our textbook for painting a positive picture of John Smith, for example, I turn to *The People's History*, by Howard Zinn, to paint the opposing picture. The picture painted of Christopher Columbus is even more slanted as he is consistently portrayed as heroic. In Zinn we learn how he sent young indigenous Central American boys with a mandate to return with gold. When they returned without it, he cut off their forearms! Students learn quickly in my class that no stone will be unturned to see that the people's history will be respected. Literature of the Americas will not be turned over to the propaganda of textbook panderers. The freshmen are encouraged to learn about the Bible in the context of history. They learn that the original Old Testament was written in Aramaic, the New Testament in Greek, and fifty years after the life of Jesus of Nazareth. There is much to encourage students to learn about the lies they have been told.

By high school, the misconceptions are quite exaggerated. There are few social science teachers willing to acknowledge that the Revolutionary War could have been prevented. It is exciting to encourage thinking about the futility and indeed, obsolescence of war. A unit of war and human relationships can bring light through literature on the effects of war and encourage research into its prevention. Sharing information called counter-recruitment, information freely afforded by the San José Peace Center, was one of my proudest accomplishments. As I watched recruiters openly lie to our students, I provided brochures explaining things that should be considered before enlisting, and explained that if a young person enlisted, they had to literally sign their body into the service. Recruiters were under no obligation to tell the truth, yet young people had to tell the truth to the recruiters; that fact exposed the injustice of recruiting techniques. As my husband is a former Marine, I could speak about many situations the students may not have considered. Occasionally he could get away to come and speak to the students directly. He spoke so sincerely about his experiences! Among my most proud moments in teaching were his visits. He explained to students, "I was a flower child before I entered the Corps, I was a flower child while I was in the Corps, and I am a flower child today. I believe in Love, Peace, and Happiness." He had their rapt attention, and they were hearing for the first, and perhaps the last time, that one could be in the military and not support unjust wars. The path to conscientious objection is often a matter of learning that the path is open.

Lately there has been great controversy over teacher evaluations and merit pay for teachers who can improve student test scores. All of it is hooey. Good teaching is not measured that way. There are so many intangibles in teaching, especially in English. As Martin Brandt, a great teacher who taught both of my girls, once wrote, "I never had a student come back and tell me how grateful they were that they did so well on their California High School Exit Exam, or their STAR test. I have, however, had them tell me how much they appreciated being encouraged to think for themselves."

Once a young *science* teacher told a student of mine that he should go into AP English because he would be "wasting his time" in my class. I phoned that teacher and gave him a piece of my mind. First of all, even if the student were misplaced into a regular English class, it was up to my discretion and experience to determine this. As it happened, I would have recommended his acceleration anyway. Second, I explained emphatically, even if he did spend a year in my class, into which many, many gifted students opted, it would *still* be a college prep class. Students sometimes decided that they wished to forego the joys of AP English their junior year. They could opt to take my regular English III class, and if they were standouts in ability or just gifted divergent thinkers, I would refer them into AP English their senior year. With few exceptions, the students I referred did well in AP Literature, so their detour was not costly. Third, and most importantly, spending a year with *me,* in and of it*self* would be reason enough to stay. Just getting to know *me* and my life story *would be an experience worth having.* I didn't back off, and the teacher shuffled a little to sound as though he hadn't meant what he had said.

Staff Transgressions

The classic episode about training students about sexual harassment on *South Park,* where they use Sexual Harassment Panda, very pointedly demonstrates some of the ill-conceived programs outside educators bring to schools. Time after time it has been shown that the top-down attitude of the adults in the environment is the key factor. If you have a culture of staff tolerance for sexually inappropriate behavior, you will find some students will push the envelope and try to get away with as much sexually inappropriate behavior as they can. If they are not called on it right away, this becomes the culture of the school. Conversely, a zero-tolerance policy on all harassment of adults to adults will help create a better climate for students as well.

My Examples of Top-down Lack of Respect

>   1.   A student advisor called me "that big gorilla" to my students—also, Big Bird
>   2.   A student advisor said, as my skirt got pulled by the computer lab door, "Wish I woulda seen that." – Response: "Excuse me! We are trying to teach these boys how to act around us, and here you are setting that *terrible example? That is not OK!*"

3.   A summer school principal announced at a faculty meeting that the student advisor was going to be checking on students' cleavage (wink wink) – Response: I told the student advisor it was his fault for letting the summer school principal say that. "How would your wife and daughter feel if they heard that?"

4.   I saw a married administrator drunk in public, in the daytime on the sidewalk outside my little girl's dance studio, walking behind a waitress while grabbing the waitress' waistline and ogling her behind

5.   The same administrator said, as I squeaked when I banged my thigh trying to get out of my auditorium seat: "Oh, I know someone who can massage that." – Response: "If I *ever* hear you talk to me like that again, I am going to charge you with sexual harassment."

6.   A teacher used sexual innuendo about my being up on a ladder – Response: "That is *not acceptable – do not ever talk to me like that again.*"

7.   Married male staff members placed bets on who could get the young blonde summer school teacher to go out with them.

8.   My first principal tried to hug me in a closed office – Response: stuck my briefcase up between us forcefully. (The same married principal was caught in a sting going to a young teacher's hotel room – he was fired, but later hired at a different district.)

9.   *A white male English teacher read out, "To be Young, Gifted and Black," adding, "Oh, that's an oxymoron," and then, "Oh. I forgot you are sensitive about that kind of stuff." – Response: Yelled: "Are you kidding me?!"*

10.   A Chinese female teacher said, "Oh, I didn't know your husband was a nih___" and stopped herself. – Response: My aide, Ms. A. Lee, was in the office with me, a beautiful, strong, young Black girl. She yelled out,

"Yeah, he *Black*!" with tears streaming down her face and laughing so hard she had to leave the room! From the look on the teacher's face, it was clear she realized that she was being laughed *at*, not with.

11.   I was informed by a campus liaison that I had not been treated well at Overfelt because I married a Black man.

12.   A white English teacher told me that with Affirmative Action, she didn't get a job because, as she put it, "*I* wasn't married to a god-damned Black man."

13.   I told an English Department Co-Chair that I heard in his college days, he had been a bit of a flower child. He backpedaled and disclaimed it immediately. I remember his co-chair's saying, "We used to shoot hippies in Wyoming." I often imagined meeting up with her in a dark alley and jacking her up, after that comment.

14.   Teachers were caught making insulting remarks about me to each other (forgetting the speakerphone was still on). – Response: Looked one woman straight in the eye while passing and re-stating to her what I had heard. "Oh, so you think I'd lose my head if it weren't screwed on?"

15.   Teachers were sometimes caught making insulting remarks about me to students, not realizing the students had more loyalty to me than to them. A math teacher told them the peace protest was "a day late and a dollar short" because I organized it. (I didn't even know about it.) – Response: Confronted teacher privately and insisted that he *never* speak to students about me again.

16.   Staff members, a bookroom clerk and career center tech, were also caught making insulting remarks about me to students, not realizing the students had more loyalty to me than to them. I always found out. The student went to ask for a

French textbook, as I had promised to tutor her in French. The bookroom clerk told her, "I can't give you that. Mrs. Demerson doesn't know any *French.*" – Response: Took clerk behind the bookroom shelves, stood *really* close (I'm 6 feet tall in shoes and she's short) and told her from now on, communication between us will be in sealed envelopes. If I ever heard about her saying *one single word* about me to another student, I would be taking it to her boss (whom she idolized).

17.   Later the same clerk was hired at the continuation school where I was teaching—as a temp —and apparently thought she could get away with this one to a student, *again*: "Oh, Demerson works here? We were so glad when she left Overfelt." The young lady ran to my classroom to tell me all about it. – Response: I marched into the front office and told the principal, "Please, bring this lady and let us step into your office for a Private Chat. Because I don't want anybody out here to hear what I have to say." The urgency in my voice convinced her to do so. When the three of us were inside, I asked her to close the door and then lit into the clerk, yelling, "I told you at Overfelt, I *warned you that if I ever heard that you talked about me to students again, it would be all over.* (She feebly tried to protest) *No, don't even try it, you know the student told me or I wouldn't be here. You know you did it. And now I'm telling you again, I'm not having it!"* Then I turned to the principal and left it in her hands. She began to assure the hapless woman that her behavior would not be tolerated. By the looks on the faces of the office staff, it was clear that they had heard me. what else could the principal do? I had called on her professionalism as well. She had to step up and supervise. Don't leave any wiggle room if you are righteous.

18.   A career center tech told me I could not use the video camera that was there for staff use. "Because we don't let everyone use it." – Response: I took it from the associate principal's office anyway, since he was the one who had told me to sign it out from the tech. *In the middle* of my students' final exam presentation requiring the video camera, the associate principal sent the activities director to take it away from me!

19.   An African American staff member refused to be associated with the Black Student Union because of me, even though I only became advisor because there *weren't any* Black teachers and the students asked me to, knowing my husband is Black. (One associate principal said, "I'm not Black, I'm Puerto Rican.") She and a student advisor were standing with their hands on their hips, staring down at us and our food, refusing to sit down with us and eat at our Thanksgiving meal, even though they had been invited and the students offered them special seats. In response, they just stood there, arms folded across their chests, glaring in disapproval for several moments, and then left.

20.   A female associate principal talked with police officers about blow jobs in the gym foyer as I was selling tickets to the game. I left the area feeling incensed and sickened.

21.   Staff members organized pudding wrestling for fundraiser (girl students included). They also tried to have a bikini car wash for the girls. I reported to the principal and got it stopped.

22.   A male staff member had girls sit on his lap poolside.

23.   A male activities director let girl cheerleaders change clothes in his classroom while he was there.

24.   Male staff members wore balloons for breasts in cross-dressing Halloween costumes (they were

mocking women, not coming out as transgender).

25.   Male and female staff members wore Bill Clinton and Monica Lewinsky costumes for Halloween.

26.   Female staff member dressed as Santa and had teen boys sit in her lap at Christmas assembly.

27.   Teacher dressed in Blackface for Halloween.

These are not all the things teachers and students experience as staff transgressions. But you get the picture. I encourage *all* new teachers to firmly communicate that they are not to be taken for granted nor remarked upon in any sexual way, ever—unless they are encouraging a bona-fide relationship with a potential spouse of an appropriate age and single status, of course. We have had lots of young staff members meet on the job and marry. That's different, and the way someone can *tell* it's different, is if *you give permission.* It is imperative that female teachers "school" the men in their workplaces in no uncertain terms and with courage of her convictions. *Just say no to sexual references.* Be polite but firm, and let the harasser know that if it *ever* happens again, their supervisor will be notified *immediately*.

For us women (and sometimes men), that is often extremely difficult to do. We have been taught to be quiet about such things; embarrassing things are best left to go away by themselves, right? Well that is why they keep happening. As my husband explained, "*All* men are dogs. It is our nature. If you do not tell us where to step off, we *will* try to get away with some shit." Then if you let it go on, you are cutting the throats of the women who come after you.

I finally overcame my hesitation to speak out. During the Senate confirmation hearings, Anita Hill spoke out about sexual harassment she suffered from aspiring Supreme Court Justice, Clarence Thomas. I understood why she never spoke up at the time, twenty years earlier, but many women who had to face

Thomas' nonsense after that might have been spared *if* she could have done something earlier. These guys' bad behaviors have to be nipped in the bud. We are the only ones who can do it, because we are the ones who are affected. Do you really think guys (or even crude women) will edit themselves? Very, very few, because it's part of the culture of patriarchy, and it is reinforced in every beer commercial, sporting event, and "man cave" mentality TV program. And by the (former) President. There is a strip-joint scene in every Hollywood movie, and pole dancing is becoming mainstream. How can women be seen as other than playthings in the workplace? With *solidarity*—phone a friend for courage if you have to—and a *no-nonsense* response to any and *all* sexual harassment. Do it for yourself, practice your affirmation in the mirror, get ready to say the actual words: "STOP. If you do that *ever* again, I will be reporting your actions to a superior." Then drop the mic like a boss and walk away. You might find yourself blushing and stammering, but you will get 'er done. Keep a written record of serious transgressions, and make sure you back them up. We had a file on one male who harassed our teen girls at Foothill Continuation School. It was a paper file, which he stole. He was not held accountable, and got to retire unscathed.

There were instances where male teachers were treated unfairly as well. One colleague was repeatedly singled out for drop-in observation and treated to rude comments by administrators, even though his dedication to his very difficult special education students was exemplary. He was repeatedly assigned classes outside of his teaching area and given little recourse despite the illegality of the assignment. My own student teacher was given an assignment of extremely difficult behavior-problem students and given very little support with classroom management training. His many gifts for working with young people were disregarded, and he was summarily fired during probationary teaching. But not only fired—kept from being hired, by agreement, in another district! To be fired is one thing, but to be blacklisted in another huge district and not given a chance to start elsewhere with a clean slate is a horse of a different color.

I protested, but by that time in my career, I felt my words of support meant nothing to the current principals. They had been abetted in their disrespect by a teacher who "ratted" on the student teacher when she saw that he, more than once, had students standing outside his classroom door. If they had had those particular students to deal with in their first year of teaching, I dare say they would have grasped at any strategy whatsoever to keep them from tearing the classroom environment to shreds and taking over. I know—they almost did it to me. Remember the corral? Luckily, I had tenure by the time I had my worst students and got away with my unorthodox kicking-out of students. There were principals who supported, and other principals who make up their minds who is in the "in crowd," and who has to go. And it is often a matter of arbitrary and capricious decision-making. The most frequent reason people are fired is because they don't get along with the boss. This is no different in teaching. To break a probationary teacher, one only has to withdraw support and assign the worst students. A recipe for failure. If you don't like your new kid on the block, treat him the way they treated my student teacher. He may be a diamond in the rough, but you will never see that because your mind was made up, and you didn't bother with the facts.

On the Warpath

I believe it is important to respect those who respect me. I would like to say that some administrators truly understand good teaching when they see it, and will support their teachers with the attitude, "We are in this together." I served under many, many principals and associate principals during my teaching years. A few principals made the grade. Alicia Mendeke, Mr. G., and Mr. M. seemed to 'get' that when you ask teachers or department chairs what *they* need to make it work, they will show their loyalty in countless ways. When they are supported both materially and with a kind word here or there, most teachers are so surprised and grateful that their performance picks up and their willingness to do all that grinding work improves. It is as true for teachers as it is for students. A campus where the principal behaves as the principal *teacher* is a campus where teachers are valued for their insight and given opportunities to decide for themselves the types of training that will best improve their practices. After a quick turnaround of principals from 1991 to 1997, I saw for the first time what a principal could be like who respected his teachers.

The year Mr. M. was to become principal at Yerba Buena, I asked for a meeting before school started. I wanted to tell him where I stood and make no bones about it. As a parent whose own mixed-race daughters had been schooled in East Side, we had lived near Yerba Buena and three blocks from Overfelt for almost twenty years, I had a vested interest in our district. I had a reason to think we could be an A school, while too many had settled for our being B-minus. In one major project, I had given students a platform, and believed they should be heard. I was somewhat surprised to hear him say, "That was *you?*" I didn't realize it had circulated to other principals.

That incident happened like this: One year the administration had changed the dress code to one of common dress: khaki, white, and green colors only. Once I asked my fashion maven daughter what she thought about school uniforms. She said, "I'd like it if the school had uniforms. If I get to pick the uniform, and it changes every day!" Gotta love that. But ostensibly, the proposed code would cut down on gang members' finding solidarity with their colors. Since gang members always find ways to identify each other anyway, I held little respect for the code. Yet, since our staff had been given a vote, and the majority had voted to implement, I enforced it. Supposedly parents had been consulted and agreed as well, although the vote could hardly have been called representative, so few parents had been actually voted. The year before one associate principal had implemented a no hats policy. She and I were standing outside on a lovely day, looking out over the student body on a break, inhabiting the quad area and other grassy knolls, a peaceful and colorful scene of youth being themselves. The associate principal said, "Doesn't that look great?" I was about to say, "I know, our kids are marvelous," when she continued, "No hats." My jaw dropped. What she saw that made her day were kids with no hats. A symbol of her power to regulate. What I saw that made my day were kids. Between the two of us, there would be no meeting of the minds or spirits about the philosophy of school. The next year, dress code was taken farther to include the no colors policy. Because frankly, khaki and white are non-colors. (I liked the green, though.)

As the first year of the common dress policy swung into effect, my second period class was grumbling although since the teachers were pretty consistent in enforcement, they were coming to school in common dress. But a kid from that class was attacked by gang member who had stuck a knife blade in his shoe. He kicked my student with the blade repeatedly, and the student was injured badly. *While* they were both wearing khaki and white. In the eyes of the students, they saw the dress code as a violation of their right to personal expression, and no deterrent whatsoever to gang violence. As discussions continued, it became clear they were also disgusted with some other campus malfunctions, the condition of the bathrooms being a major complaint. After their fellow student was stabbed, the class erupted with complaining and yelling about how the school didn't really care about them. This went on for two days, and my lesson plan was out the window from the disruption. This was a Composition and Literature class, and the students' reading and writing skills were perfunctory at best. So as an exercise to vent, I asked them to write their concerns about the dress code, the bathrooms, and anything else, in proper typewritten letters, and I promised to make sure they were given out to all the adults in their environment who might be able to do something about it. I worked with them in the computer lab as they composed, word-processed, and then signed their letters. Most of them were so upset about the common dress they were spitting mad, but it seemed they had finally calmed down and had begun to turn resentment into protest.

I had told them that if they were organized, they might be able to accomplish something, but random yelling was getting them nowhere. I explained that in my high school, led by me and others who thought as I did, that our dress code was mindless and sexist, two hundred of us sat on the cafeteria floor until the principal agreed to change the dress code to allow girls to wear pants, and boys to have long hair, among other changes. The condition was that their parents had to sign a waiver stating that they would not sue the school if their kid was attacked for wearing whatever they chose. The behavior manual had always said that if the clothing did not disrupt the class, it was acceptable. So when I tested my new freedom and wore a pantsuit to class, my algebra teacher tried to stop me at the door. I told him my clothing was to be permitted as it would not disrupt the class. He told me to put my algebra homework problem on the chalkboard, and if it did not disrupt the class, he would allow it. I did, and nobody batted an eyelash. We had won our case with civil disobedience. I told the students that if they had a 2.0 grade point average and good attendance, they could get a waiver at the district office to wear whatever they wanted, but since they didn't do that, then they were stuck with what the school had voted to support. I explained that I did not agree with a common dress code, but that I was a professional, and I agreed to comply with what my colleagues had decided upon. "What if I went to your job and told you to violate your boss' rules, when you might catch hell as a result?"

The noise did not subside as the students were adamant that they all knew who the gangsters were, that everyone could tell who was who because of the way they carried themselves and the *way* they wore their clothing, so what did having common dress do to help them? All it did was punish the students who did nothing wrong. So when they completed their letters, I, true to my word, copied them on my own dime at the local copy store, put them into my own envelopes, and sent them out using my own stamps to every school board member, the superintendent, the principal, the associate principal, every single teacher and staff member in our school, and the head of our parent association. I listed the return address as simply "Demerson," and my school address. I got a call from a male board member asking me who I was and what those were for. I explained the situation and my promise to the students. He seemed upset and thought that I was trying to remain anonymous. I simply stated that I did not write the letters, the students who signed them wrote them. A female board member sent an email to the principal and it stated: "Get those YB bathrooms cleaned *now*."

The associate principal and principal called me in to their office. The associate principal was angry and ranted about what kind of ideas I was giving my students. She, of course, was in charge of the school campus and discipline, so it was a referendum on her performance. I didn't expect her to be happy. I told them that these were the honest outpourings of the students. I told them that I thought every adult in their environment should have the opportunity to help. I invited them to come to the class and speak with the students to explain their points of view. The associate principal said, "You are teaching these students, what? That if they don't like something, they can write a *letter* about it?"

Exactly! She refused to come to the classroom and said that she had been blindsided. Both the principal and the associate principal asked why I didn't come to them and ask their permission.

I said, "Would you have let me send the letters?"

They said, "No."

"Well, that's why I didn't ask."

The associate principal called the parents in to the school to talk about the letters. She tried to blame me and said that I had been putting forth my own agenda. The parents were not fooled. They said things like, "You are missing the point. My kid wrote that letter: That's her signature on the bottom."

It didn't get the common dress code repealed, but it did get the bathrooms cleaned. The class felt vindicated and listened to. I felt victorious on the students' behalf. I never heard another word about it, except from other teachers who complimented the action. They tried to say I was brave, but I really hadn't thought I had anything to lose. I knew they didn't like me in the front office anyway. I just wanted to help some young people learn that the word processor can be mightier than the blade in the shoe. Or at least, that they can express themselves and be heard. I kept stacks of these letters in my drawer and took them out from time to time over the years, to remember to give students a voice.

So the new principal knew from our first meeting at Yerba Buena that I stood for what I believed. During the course of his tenure at Yerba Buena, I saw many, many examples of his respect for the teachers. I was especially surprised at how much one could be willing to do for a principal who works as hard as the teachers and respects the students as well. Once the same associate principal who had objected to teaching the kids to write letters kept asking us to hand-carry our roll sheets to the office every day. My classroom was across a very large campus, and I rarely had a moment to myself, so going on my little fifteen-minute break to the attendance office was a pain in the butt. All the previous years of my teaching, I had confidently sent the attendance with a student, and only once was the trust violated as a girl changed the attendance mark of absent to present for her boyfriend. I was even willing to take the attendance documents halfway, to the faculty lounge mailbox, where I could at least get a chance to use the restroom during my break. When she called me one more time to insist that I hand-carry the documents to her office, I finally just stated, "I just can't do it. It's just too illogical." She reported my actions to Mr. M., thinking I would get in trouble. Mr. M. told her, "That's OK, I will pick them up and bring them to you." Wha...? What principal supports his teachers like that? Letting her know that the teacher is to be respected, that the other members of staff are really there to support *our* efforts. That was the best encouragement a principal could give. He did, in fact, walk over to pick them up and deliver them, and I never, ever walked attendance documents to the office.

I continued to work very hard to be a cooperative curriculum leader. When a new requirement would be placed on our department, he and his *other* associate principal would consult with me and ask me what our department needed in order to get this done. How different from the other principals, who merely told teachers what we *had* to do. It made us feel valued and supported.

A little respect top-down can really galvanize a faculty. During Mr. M.'s years, Yerba Buena received a six-year full accreditation from the Western Association of Schools and Colleges, who accredit schools for the state. It is rare for a school like Yerba Buena to receive such an accreditation, as it means they will not be observed by teams for another six years and are in fact trusted to continue their good work. I think being trusted to do good work is what motivates everyone in a school. How is it that principals and teachers don't trust more and criticize less?

Schools that have an in-crowd mentality, where some teachers are clearly pets or lackeys of the administration. Some teachers get their pick of students, for example, in schools where there is favoritism. One science teacher I worked with was given the right of interviewing prospective students for the Advanced Placement Environmental Science class, picking and choosing his own class. Conversely, they took away my prior right to administer writing samples for incoming freshmen in order to place them more accurately in English classes at their levels. Some teachers get rewards and praise in assemblies and faculty meetings, while others continue to work small miracles, unsung. One physiology teacher, Sujata Lal, held a phenomenal record-breaking blood drive each year yet was required to practically beg for the space in the gym to set it up! I don't remember her ever having been given any special reward nor even recognition for this. In fact, she was being given less and less desirable schedule assignments as she became more and more experienced. Many of us teachers recognized that ageism was at play.

If principals remember that bullying and favoring students doesn't work in the classroom, they could also remember it doesn't work coming from the front office. Alas, administrators are human beings, flawed like the rest of us, and their office neither guarantees trustworthiness nor capacity for leadership. I have met the good, the bad, and the ugly, and most of the administrators I've known were at best merely competent. The good went unheralded for the most part, just as in teaching, but they don't do it for acclaim. They share a common vision with the good teachers, and they work long hours year-round to help improve their schools. I shall always remember Mr. M. the first time I saw him at Yerba Buena, out at seven in the morning picking up trash in front of the administration building. I teased him with a smile, "What in the hell are you doing?" as we proceeded in for our first meeting. Champion administrators are accountable fiscally and personally. When a principal takes the attitude, "The buck stops here. When outcomes are questioned, I will hold myself personally accountable to the community for the actions of the staff, the adults in this environment, as well as the students," then we have a leader.

Some Hope, Some Successes, Something to Look Forward To

All in all, a school is a microcosm of the world in which it finds itself. The milieu of the school will in large part determine what *could* take place inside the campus. The neighborhood suggests a certain culture that will need to be considered by all staff, especially those who live outside of the neighborhood, and who visit the campus after commuting from their various other living situations. If we look at how many teachers don't recognize gang signs, for example, or never bother to learn the most basic greetings in students' home languages, or never try to find cultural relevance for students in their subject matter, we have problems. We have performance gaps for African-American and Latino students in nearly every school. White and Asian students tend to score more highly on standardized tests. Is this because many of the Black and Brown students are part of a system that relies on a permanent underclass to perform its most manual and perfunctory jobs? We can establish a clear link between income, race, and SAT scores. We can establish that third generation Mexican and Central American immigrants, as well as those Asian and other immigrants who have no firm grounding in their home language will also struggle in English. We can demonstrate that learning a new language to the level of one's peers who have always spoken English at home will take five to six years. Yet we continue to wonder, "Why the achievement gap?" It becomes most significant and most imperative that new teachers learn to find ways to motivate students whose performance and subsequent successes are *dependent* upon their motivation. I can be as excited as I want to be about my subject matter, but when a student doesn't read one word of the novel nor pick up a pen to write one word, I can hardly say my excitement meant a damn thing. So where do I begin?

The very first imperative is research on the milieu. Where do the kids live? What is the language spoken at home? What cultural connections can they bring to the table? Asking open-ended questions during a novel reading: "Have you ever heard of _____?" Or expecting that someone may have, in fact, seen a chicken having its head twisted off (as in *Rain God*). Assume that what someone in the class can explain is going to be listened to with more rapt attention than what any teacher might say. Remember that to them, we sometimes sound like the teacher in the Charlie Brown movie, "Wah wah wah wah wah…"

Have a plethora of different reading and studying methods at the ready and give them some choices among them. At the beginning of the year, teach the methods by explaining them clearly and giving directional handouts. Have students model the strategy for their peers. This is key. There is considerably more buy-in when students see their peers participating with confidence. One day might find my students doing reciprocal reading; the next interactive journals in pairs; the third day making something hands on; the fourth watching a teacher-centered PowerPoint presentation with music which they may relax and enjoy, perhaps taking Cornell notes. By Friday there may be quick quizzes—done in pen so that they can grade each others'—in order to cut down the grading workload.

Remember that logistical tasks can be done by students. My job is very difficult. Why would I ever do something that a student can do better than I can? All that clerical stuff can be supervised and given to student assistants who love to help. Would you really like to grade 150 spelling tests? If not, it can be done better by student assistants. You do need to oversee, but your work will go faster, and students will take pride in accomplishment. They will also feel that you have trusted them as adults if you give them opportunities and rewards for helping. My students loved cash. Even a little made a big difference. You must grade essays and more critical tests, so don't think you are getting off easy!

Ask them to fill their backpacks of life with the best strategies with which to go forward. Teach them what worked for you. Have them demonstrate for each other how they study for other classes. Create study-buddy teams for those who want a peer to help them get caught up when they have missed class. Help your students to help each other whenever possible. Reward individuals within groups separately, even if there is a group product. Everybody hates being graded down for the laziness of another group member.

In short, be a professional studier of students. Their learning life is your responsibility, at least with the curriculum of your area of study. The least you can do is try to figure out how they are learning best, play to that strength, and at the same time, offer scaffolding to more complex and sophisticated study strategy. Take every course you can in classroom management. The little tips are sometimes the biggest lifesavers.

Pick your worst student, the one you never want to see again, the one who, when you see is *absent*, your heart feels happy. Then make that student your best friend. Sit him or her next to you and praise, praise, praise the good behavior. Learn the different areas of intelligence: who is strong in what area and give them projects that allow for their strengths to shine through. Be wary of the word "rigor," and remember that it often just means "more work," rather than more purposive work with more depth and complexity. What can a student learn in a twenty-page research paper that he or she could not learn in ten? Most likely more plagiarism, certainly more grading for you. Offer more than one topic for writing assignments to give students choices for expression. Believe in your heart that what they have to say is important. I encourage teachers of other subjects to collaborate for more writing assignments across the curriculum. Try to pair with someone who is not in your subject area. *Get training in brain research from someone outside of the field of education!* The way students learn now is demonstrably different than the way many of us teachers learned, in the actual function of the brain. Knowing about the latest research will fine-tune your pedagogy.

The Ethnic Project

Every year for many, many years, I used the American Literature course to demonstrate to students that the literature of their own ethnic group is a part of our American tapestry. "Literature is the Cultural Language of Our Human Family" was a banner above my desk. If a teacher wishes to engage students from where they are and take them to where they can be, it helps to cultivate self-knowledge. The project I incorporated was once controversial at Overfelt, where the administration didn't seem to think I taught enough writing by dead white men. They disapproved, in no uncertain terms, of the Ethnic Project for the honors students. I was not deterred, and I continue to advocate for the study of ethnic authors. Picture a meeting where I am disqualified by the associate principal from teaching Honors English III because the department chairperson, even though he had asked me to teach it in the first place to coordinate across the curriculum with American History for juniors, then claimed that I was teaching with a bias. Oh, yes, I did explain that the oldies and goodies were being covered – did they not consider Hawthorne, Melville, Emerson, Thoreau to be white enough? The Jewish department chair actually said that his mentor had once told him not to teach the literature of the holocaust because he would teach it with a bias. I exclaimed, "But Rob! Your being Jewish makes you particularly qualified to teach the holocaust!" I went home to explain my angst to my husband, to which he replied angrily, "All great teachers come from a bias! Martin Luther King had a *bias!* Mahatma Gandhi had a *bias!*"

The Ethnic Project includes every ethnicity of the students in my classes, even the rare Italian or Swedish or Swiss or Australian student I found in my predominantly non-white schools. (Sometimes schools where I taught had foreign exchange students from Europe. They received quite an education and were always encouraged in my class to share their cultural experiences as well.) There is a book for everyone. These books are proven to make connections for students. My strategy was to ask the students to group according to their own ethnicity yet make it clear that they were free to join any other group of their choice. Sometimes a student would be the only student in his or her group, and that would be OK, too. On some days during the project, they would be asked to work with another group because the activity required more than one person.

On the first day, the students would learn the name and author of their book and were given several ways to get their hands on the book. These included the bookroom or library if the school carried it, online sellers—and I was happy to order for them with my teacher's discount, or sometimes they could buy a copy from someone who took my course the previous year. If none of the books I had on the list matched their ethnicity, I'd go online with that student and find a book by an American author of that ethnicity. The hardest one to find has been Swiss-American, since Swiss-Americans simply identify as American. But find one we did. I encouraged the students to buy the paperbacks themselves, so they could keep them and share them with family members. Some students' families were so excited to see a book by, for example, a Cambodian-American author, that they would immediately try to borrow the book before the student was finished with it. If a student did not have the money to buy the book and it was not available at the library or bookroom, I would take up a collection to help those who could not pay. It was quick work to get fifty cents from thirty students, giving a student a fifteen-dollar book. At the end of several weeks of study and activities, each group of students presented their book to the rest of the class and made a presentation of culture including food, dress, music, and art. Usually, the presentations came at the end of the term. I always gained five pounds that week as I couldn't turn down the food made by students or their parents. I offered to reimburse the moms who made food for the project. Most often, they would refuse the money, and were happy to contribute with pride.

It was always so exciting to hear the students' reactions to their books. Many students over the years have burst into spontaneous crying while trying to explain the sacrifices their parents made to bring them here to the United States, as evidenced by the experiences of the characters in the books they have read. They cried when they tell how they, too, have lost a cousin to gang violence. One family actually knew the author of a book about the Cambodian-American experience, *To Destroy You is No Loss,* and they were so enthralled by the book that my student had a hard time getting it back from various family members in time to read for class. Sometimes I would take a reluctant group to the library and begin reading aloud to them. Once while reading the beginning of *America is in the Heart* to some rowdy Filipino boys, I noticed they started crying in the first chapter. From that experience, they were hooked. During the final presentations, we laughed and ate and enjoyed each other's' cultures. I always encouraged them to ask the questions they'd always wanted to know about each other's' ethnicities. They had to read the book to get to the final presentation, and almost all of them did.

Every day I encouraged a new approach as to how to share the experience of reading. They read alone and reflected in writing. They read aloud to each other. They read and wrote poetry about what they had read. They read and refined their writing about their reading. They worked on computers together to create PowerPoint presentations. They cooked, they served, they dressed up. In the end, everyone got a "taste" of one another's cultures and experiences, fraught with struggle, defeat, and ascendance.   At the end of each year when we had exit conferences, the Ethnic Project received the highest approval rating of any of the projects I have done with students.

Exit conferences using the portfolio of writings students have done over their high school years is a very useful tool. Ask questions that evoke reflections, such as, "What skill do you see has improved the most from your freshman to your senior year?" "What writing project did you learn the most from?" "What did you like the best about my class, and what do you think I could improve for next year's students?"

Students have returned from university in subsequent years to express their appreciation. One girl said, "I never really thought about what it means to be Mexican until I read the books in your class. It started me on a path of self-discovery and made me confident enough to think I could be successful in college."

One student wrote a tribute that rewarded my persistence in acknowledging the student's worth. He won the local Barnes and Noble essay contest for a teacher appreciation essay. It reminded me of what a precarious relationship exists between our students and their world; how marvelous it can be to be appreciated; how vital it can be to have faith in the faithless.

I hesitate to include the letter, as it sounds self-congratulatory. But to all the teachers in public schools who give of themselves to public service with authentic energy and heart, this is for you:

A thank you letter by JH
Dear,
Describe Her?
Five Hundred words, one thousand hand chiseled hieroglyphics symbols, one million alphabetical letters, somehow meaningless.
Even actions derived by means of work and sweat alone cannot fully unearth past deeds of this over-looked saint.
Thus, charity unselfish by nature does not harden human form angels from shedding tears over tragic, desperate tales...

To begin...

To live...

To die...

To live a life for personal gain is sweet and simple, to live for others through their trials, their own personal holocaust is just asking for an early retirement or a 6-foot-tall, 3-foot-wide, wooden box.

To try to become the solution not just for one but to a handful of angry, "economically challenged" high school students is what the Congress, or Senate would state as "Virtually impossible!"

I'm not a straight A student nor a B grade average nor do I even possess a GPA suitable for such parental praise.

I was an incoming freshman with troubles that could easily be forced into residency by one of our city's finest cold metal bars and brick castle.

I was a drunk that could easily empty out a tavern of its brew, spirits, and fine light and dark liquor.

I was notorious, at such an early stage in life that I was viewed by others as reckless, and overall too dangerous to cross swords with.

Life to me apparently was just one big video game with no ending credits.

Thus, I was the outcast: the Venus flytrap in a greenhouse of roses, tulips, and buzzing bees.

I was just another angry, stubborn idiot with a big knife.

Ultimately, being shot at, running from the law, drinking till I blacked out are just another page in my life.

For four years she struggled every 8-hour day to convince me that I was too intelligent to end up in a county jail or in some random alley lying face down, or in a crowded dumpster.

So

Guidance is what she offered me, and in return she asked for nothing but the seed of my success.

Thank you.

With help I prospered, bloomed.
Thus, success is the fruit I bear.
Because...
She is my mentor, the cause of my rise, the wood for my burning motivation.
With her I learn my life was mine to hold and cherish...
All these remarkable compliments, praise, deeds belong to one and I mean one remarkable, unique woman that educates English students at a college level skill at Yerba Buena High School. Mrs. Demerson is a living testament that all challenges can be overcome, that any dreams can be reached, that anyone can be successful. I am the proof of her teachings, the troubled boy who grew into a man, a man that is starting a new life as an educated student, a man going to college instead of a bar.
Thank You, Mrs. Demerson.

The Denouement

This experiment in life, in being incarnated as a human being on planet Earth, is truly terrifying and truly awe-inspiring. I tell my students on the last day before each holiday break and summer: "I know that while everyone else celebrates, sometimes holidays are the very worst times for us. Some of us are not looking forward to a happy time away from here. My heart is with you. I believe we were put on Earth to help each other. What other possible reason could there be? So if you know someone who is going home to a *bad* situation, get their number now, and touch base with them over the break."

Once a white student of mine was mocking a Filipino student's accent. I sent him out on the porch because I was so mad at him. We heard the portable classroom banging, and I went outside to find someone had come along and beat him up! He left a suicide note on his desk that day. I was guilt-ridden and worried, so I called the guidance office. The counselor said he was going home for the weekend and there was nothing to be done about it! I asked if any of the students could check on him this afternoon. An African-American boy said he knew where he lived and promised to stop by his house and check on him. They both returned on Monday. I never forgot that and reminded all my students to look out for one another.

As we "wait for the messiah," or as we just struggle to get through high school, why not, as *Educating Hearts and Minds* suggests, involve young people in their own destiny?

"Define the problems, Brainstorm possible solutions, Evaluate the solutions, Decide on a solution to try, Determine how to implement the decision, and Evaluate the solution." [viii]

The wise teacher understands the power of this method as a class meeting tool, and uses it to prevent discord, no matter the challenges of teaching every single student who walks through the door. In public schools we have the greatest opportunity and the greatest mandate. America's public schools were first instituted in Massachusetts in the early 1600s, and I believe they remain to this day our greatest accomplishment.

In the 1990s, in a Republican Governor's term, he tried to implement a policy requiring public school teachers to report on the immigration status of our students. We flatly refused. Teachers are neither ICE nor police. We are teachers. And now to think they are suggesting we arm ourselves with guns? We must never give up our rights to academic freedom nor acquiesce to ideas that neither benefit students nor ourselves! We can and will learn to meet the challenges of public educators for all. Dr. Montessori shows us, when the number of those behaving well reaches critical mass, they are a powerful force for cohesion in the social order and improve the self-esteem and sense of well-being of all the class members. If we genuinely believe that we teach the whole being, then this is the result most highly to be sought.

As I started this book, I remarked that the potential for change works not just within the student, but within the heart of the teacher as well. The lessons I learned from these individuals and their journeys brought such changes in the tapestry of my life, and wove within it all of the colors I dreamt of in my favorite recurring dream. It's a dream where my husband and I are leading a troupe of children, all of us riding unicycles, streaming rainbow streamers, and singing: "I see your true colors shining through/ I see your true colors, and that's why I love you./ So don't be afraid to let 'em see/ Your true colors/ True colors are beautiful...like a rainbow."[ix]

I remember many years ago being mocked by a math teacher in

the parking lot as he sang out, "We are the world" in a goofy voice. He thought the Feed the World Club was a hippie joke. Neither his sarcasm nor the taunts of the many nay-sayers and jealous curmudgeons ever stopped my dream. I dream it still.

If you decide to become a public educator even after reading this book, know that you are supported by the many who have gone before you. I am happy to send lesson plans, advice, encouragement, and commiseration to any who requests via my email: HannahLynnDemerson@gmail.com

---

[i] Hughes, Langston, "Mother to Son," Poetry Foundation. Accessed January 18, 2021.

https://www.poetryfoundation.org/poems/47559/mother-to-son.

[ii]Freire, Paulo, 1921-1997. *Pedagogy of the Oppressed.* New York: Continuum, 2000.

[iii] *Bloom's Taxonomy.* (Bloom, 1956.)
   [iv]
George Orwell, from *Why I Write.*

[v] "Ohio" by Crosby, Stills, Nash, and Young, 1970.

[vi] Shakur, T., 2021. Available at: https://www.youtube.com/watch?v=8xEL80bYlsY

   [Accessed 6 March 2021].

[vii] (*Romeo and Juliet*, ii.ii.72-73).

[viii] DeRoche, Edward F., and Mary M. Williams. *Educating Hearts and Minds: a*
   Comprehensive Character Education Framework. Corwin Press,

2001.

[ix] "True Colors" performed by Cyndi Lauper, written by Billy Steinberg and Tom Kelly.

Appendix

A Partial List of Books for the Ethnic Project

From the handout for students: "It is important to recognize that there are great American authors from your background. Reading groups for this project are based on ethnicity. I recommend you choose to study an American author of your own ethnicity, and later read one from another group. Many great thinkers have said that "All knowledge is self-knowledge." This means we try to understand ourselves and our background first, and from there we can reach out with a firm grounding when we go to understand others and the background of others. If you choose to join another group, that is fine as well."

Mexican-American Group 1
Always Running by Luis Rodriguez

Mexican-American Group 2
Rain of Gold by Victor Villasenor

Mexican-American Group 3
La Maravilla by Alfredo Vea

Vietnamese-American Group
Catfish and Mandala by Andrew X. Pham

Cambodian-American Group

To Destroy You is No Loss by Joan D. Criddle for Teeda Butt Man

Chinese-American Group 1
The Joy Luck Club by Amy Tan

Chinese-American Group 2
China Men by Maxine Hong Kingston

Filipino -American Group
America is in the Heart by Carlos Bulosan

Honduran -American Group
Don't be Afraid, Gringo by Elvia Alvarado

Salvadoran -American Group
The Weight of All Things by Sandra Benitez

Laotian -American Group
Mother's Beloved: Stories from Laos by Outhine Bounyavong

African -American Group 1
A Hope in the Unseen by Ron Suskind [a Jewish author— the story of a Black boy from one of the worst inner-city schools in the nation who makes it to Brown University]

African-American Group 2
Roots by Alex Haley

West Indian – American Group
Brown Girl, Brownstones by Paule Marshall

Fijian—American (Australian) Group
Homework by Suneeta Peres Acosta

Swiss- American Group
Rules of Deception by Christopher Reich

Basque-American Group
The Basque Hotel by Robert Laxault

Samoan-American Group
Frank: A Samoan American Odyssey by Jo A. Lord

Huichol-American Group
Earthwalks for Body and Spirit by James Endredy

Hmong-American Group
The Spirit Catches You and You Fall Down by Anne Fadiman

Italian-American Group
Christ in Concrete by Pietro di Donato

Japanese-American Group
Looking like the Enemy: My Story of Imprisonment in Japanese-American Internment Camps by Mary Matsuda Gruenewald

Nicaraguan-American Group
Hummingbird House by Patricia Henley

Indian (Asian Indian)-American group
The Gurkha's Daughter by Prajwal Parajuly

Swedish-American Group
Giants in the Earth by Ole Edvart Rølvaag

Afghan-American Group
The Kite-Runner by Khalid Hosseini
A Thousand Perfect Suns by Khalid Hosseini

Ukrainian-American Group
Souvenirs from Kyiv by Chrystyna Lucyk-Berger

Coeur d'Alene Group
The Lone Ranger and Tonto Fistfight in Heaven by Sherman Alexie

The books of other tribes available upon request: Chippewa Louise Erdrich and Joy Harjo recommended among other authors.

About The Author

Hannah Lynn Demerson

spent thirty-four years in the service of families whose children attended public schools in California. The photograph is of her mother, Mrs. Alice Hepworth Simpson, and Mrs. Demerson at her whiteboard with the same handwriting and the same lesson! It is a legacy passed down that also includes her

grandmother, Mrs. Annie P. Hepworth, and her daughter, Doctor Rainy Demerson.

She collected the stories of her teaching life to share with an increasingly curious public. It is her fervent hope that these stories will enlighten all who take an interest and encourage our future teachers to take a leap of faith into this challenging and rewarding field. She and her husband have two daughters and two grandsons. She is currently retired and living happily in the Sierra Foothills of California.

Synopsis

With the focus on public schools in our current public debate, with the threats to public education on every front, what is it really like to be a public-school teacher? This is my story. It is a memoir of a decades-long love for a career that challenges and rewards; devastates and uplifts.

I wish to let teachers, parents, students, and concerned citizens see the life of a high school classroom through my window. I want to appeal to young people who might be considering a career in public education and help them to make decisions. You never know until you have classes of your own—just how much your students can surprise, terrify, and delight you. You never really know if your experience is the same as anyone else's, or if you are in this thing alone. We need more great teachers to meet the challenges of the twenty-first century! These stories may help you understand the depth and complexity of a noble profession.

Made in the USA
Coppell, TX
30 June 2022